CONSERVATION OF BIODIVERSITY AND THE NEW REGIONAL PLANNING

Edited by

Richard E. Saunier
and
Richard A. Meganck

April 1996
warm Regards,

Department of Regional Development and Environment
Executive Secretariat for Economic and Social Affairs
General Secretariat, Organization of American States

1995

A publication of the Organization of American States and the IUCN--The World Conservation Union. Production of this work has been made possible in part by a grant from the Commission of the European Communities. The views and opinions expressed in this work do not necessarily represent those of the Commission of European Communities or other participating organizations.

LIBRARY OF CONGRESS CATALOGING-IN-PUBLICATION DATA

Conservation of Biodiversity and the New Regional Planning / edited by Richard E. Saunier and Richard A. Meganck.
ISBN 0-8270-3592-6

Cover photograph by Peter Jacobs.
Cover design by David Saunier.

1995

Commission of the European Communities

Preface

One often hears that regional planning is a thing of the past and that, for better or for worse, the current model is one of sectoral planning and the execution of isolated development projects. It is a model that separates conservation and development into opposing and combative groups, and therefore it is one that requires the strictest of environmental evaluations if conservation is to be properly considered.

In January of 1992, Richard E. Saunier and Richard A. Meganck, the editors of this volume, coordinated a workshop on *The New Regional Planning* at the IVth World Congress on National Parks and Protected Areas in Caracas, Venezuela, in which nearly 50 case studies from Africa, Asia, and North, Central, and South America showed that integrated regional-scale planning is not a thing of the past at all. And it showed that planning of this nature not only designs strategies to integrate development responses to the human needs within a region; it also includes responses to the needs of biodiversity conservation.

The outcome of the *New Regional Planning* workshop was a preliminary portrait of something that had begun to emerge with the publication of the *World Conservation Strategy* in 1980 and of the report of the World Commission on Environment and Development published in 1987. This portrait is being further filled in by efforts following the 1992 United Nations Conference on Environment and Development to formulate sustainable development criteria and standards. An evolving paradigm suggests that these criteria and standards are not solely an assortment of numbers and limits nor even new institutions and regulations--as important as these may be. Rather, as often discussed in this volume, they are embodied in a process guided by concerns that development be equitable and consensus-driven and that the planning of that development be sectorally and spatially integrated.

This book, then, is a next step in the ongoing characterization of sustainable development. It is a set of conclusions drawn from case descriptions and methods that look at the "why" and "how" of the new regional planning. Chapters 1, 2, 3 and 4 make the case for the importance of both wild and cultured biodiversity; Chapters 5, 6 and 7 give instructions on how attention can be given to special parts of the

iii

overall effort; Chapter 8 links the topic to the recently ratified *Convention on Biological Diversity*; and Chapters 9, 10 and 11 discuss experiences from the well-known cases of La Amistad International Park in Costa Rica and Panama, the Greater Yellowstone Coalition in the United States, and CAMPFIRE in Zimbabwe as they fit into the parameters of the new regional planning.

We and our institutions are proud to support the publication of this book.

Kirk P. Rodgers
Director, Department of
  Regional Development and
  Environment
Organization of American States

Thaddeus C. Trzyna
Chair, Commission on
  Environmental Strategy and
  Planning
IUCN

Acknowledgments

The Editors wish to thank the following individuals for their support and encouragement during the long process of putting this book together: Carola Saavedra, Secretary, Department of Regional Development and Environment of the Organization of American States, for making the numerous changes in the text, formatting its presentation, and keeping track of everything throughout; Trish Miller, Secretary, ManTech International, Corvallis, Oregon, for typing early versions of Chapters 2, 5, and 11; Betty Robinson for making something coherent out of what was originally presented to her; and Kathleen Ann Farley for helping to search out the references. Richard Sims of the Organization of American States managed the publication and printing activities, and he, Caroline Martinet, Penny Wallace and David Sheppard of the IUCN worked out the many problems of funding; Dr. Hermann Gucinski, Corvallis, Oregon, and Dr. Neal E. Bandlow, Morrissville, New York, helped review and edit early versions of the text; and Peter Jacobs, Professor of Landscape Architecture at the University of Montreal, provided the cover photo. We would like, also, to thank the authors of each chapter for their considerable patience and for their willingness to share their insight into the problems of conservation and development planning. Finally, we would like to thank our institutions, the Organization of American States and the United Nations Environment Programme, and IUCN and the Commission of the European Communities for providing us the opportunity to make this book possible.

R.E.S.
R.A.M.

Contents

Chapter 1

INTRODUCTION

Richard E. Saunier and
Richard A. Meganck

Two major challenges have faced the human species since it became established on planet Earth. The first of these challenges is to survive and improve our life quality without destroying the support capacity of the ecosystems we are a part of. And the second is to appropriate the services these systems provide without conflicting with others who wish to use these and other services from the same systems for different purposes. Though these challenges are little different from the ones confronting all species, mankind can respond with forethought, analysis, and conscious adjustment of behavior to a larger degree than most others.

Despite such advantages, human history abounds with examples of our failure to fully meet these challenges. Civilizations have vanished from the face of the earth leaving little except the remnants of opulence gained from the mismanagement of resources and the stories of wars fought over lands and waters that, in the end, apparently could provide neither the material nor the spiritual sustenance required by all the opposing groups.

We are, however, still here. Though civilizations have vanished, the human species survives and a greater number, perhaps even a greater percentage, of its members now have a better life than ever before. A continuing process of invention, adaptation, and discovery has allowed us to endure, expand, adapt, and conquer. Despite the many conflicts now under way, ethical constructs have evolved that save more of us from ourselves than before. Technologies have been invented that notably increase the carrying capacity of many of the ecosystems we use. And, however imperfectly, methods have been designed to manage more of these systems so that they provide more of what we require. One of these methods, which shows up in a variety of ways, is planning. And, although it pains some to hear this, perhaps the most successful of these is economic development planning.

The "success" of economic development confronts those who are interested in the conservation of biodiversity with a choice. Economic development can be rejected, perhaps, but if this is done, meaningful dialogue with those thought to be the opposition will be cut off and the full set of hoped-for conservation objectives will remain unrealized. Or we can attempt to understand and deal with the pervasiveness of economic development and its planning. After all, the words "economic development planning" are not necessarily bad. Development defined as a "process that attempts to improve life quality" is a positive thing. Economics, at its base, is a word that represents the concept of managing our home. And planning, though never making things perfect, is an honest attempt to make them better.

The New Regional Planning

There are, of course, many kinds of economic development and one of these takes place at the regional level. The world in which we find ourselves is complex, and we spend a great deal of time looking for ways to make it less so. We divide it politically, for example, in an effort to make it more governable. In the minds of many, sustainable development divides it temporally to somehow account for the future. Scientists partition its study into more specific disciplines in order to keep track of burgeoning amounts of information. Planners and users of its resources divide its manipulation into development sectors. Regional planning is a variation on this theme in which the cut is made spatially instead of sectorally (OAS, 1984).

Beyond saying that the "new regional planning" builds on the "old regional planning" and generally leaves aside the more traditional characteristics of regional planning like growth poles, centralized authority, and inflexible recommendations, figuring out the real differences between them is an interesting and necessary exercise. Doing so will help us to arrive at a workable definition of the new regional planning.

One might think for example, that the *new*, as opposed to *old*, is planning that includes "conservation areas" as one of the land-use categories of the final "regional plan." However, a major proposal of one of the early planning exercises of the Organization of American States in the rain forest of Peru looked toward the establishment of the Cutiribeni National Park (OEA, 1967b). Cutibireni only recently became an official addition to Peru's system of conservation areas; yet that study was done over 25 years ago.

Perhaps the *new* regional planning deals with integrated analysis and conservation of natural resources. But integrated natural resource surveys have been done for nearly 30 years (OEA, 1967a) and regional conservation efforts were undertaken long before that, in 1933, through the Tennessee Valley Authority (Allen, 1955). Possibly, the *new* employs high-powered computers and geographic information systems (GIS) that allow sophisticated manipulation of data, but, again, what is new here is the technology and not the method or objectives; that method was being used in the 1960s (McHarg, 1967). No, the differences do not lie in these kinds of things. They lie elsewhere, and to find them we need to look at economic development planning, see what it is about, and then look at a fundamental difference between that paradigm and the emergence of a new paradigm--the new regional planning. To summarize the first part of that exercise, there are three fundamental questions that form the bases for economic development planning: (1) What are the resources available for improving life quality? (2) How are they to be manipulated? and (3) For whom? (Samuelson, 1976).

Under what is normally thought of as economic planning, these resources are the classic natural resources: forests and other vegetation, water, soil, wildlife, minerals, atmosphere, etc. Governed by this arrangement, the development sectors decide how to manipulate the individual resource of interest to them in response to the needs of their own constituencies. For regional planning, the constituencies are the whole range of resource users in the region. Resource manipulation, however, remains in the hands of the development sectors where resources continue to be thought of as the ones listed above. Again, the differences are not significant.

What is different, however, is that a fourth economic question has been added: *Who is to decide* what the resource is, what we do with it, and for whom? "Who is to decide?" is a question that added a whole new dimension to classical economic development. How that question is answered is one of the main issues separating the old regional planning from the new. The differences exist largely because of the environmental movement and its success in advancing at least four major considerations:

3

Conservation is a development activity. That conservation should be accepted as a development activity is the first of these. The environmental movement, of course, clarified and promoted the fact that the success of the development enterprise depends, in large part, on activities of conservation (IUCN *et al.*, 1980). And, in doing so, it discovered that the reverse is also true: the success of conservation efforts also hinges on a balanced and equitable process of development (WCED, 1987). These, of course, are what make up the common elements of the many definitions of sustainable development. As a consequence, conservation activities are as much a part of the development scenario as are building a dam or constructing a utilities network.

Neighbors are important. Secondly, the environmental movement insisted that the affected populations of any development activity be included in the formulation and execution of that activity. This suggests how regional planning must deal with the neighbors of the region being planned as well as with its inhabitants. It is not enough to have all the individuals and groups that hold lands within the region involved in how the area and its resources are to be used. There are many other "neighbors" out there who have a great deal to say about how resources are managed. These include, of course, the nearby populations who have historically made use of the area or who may be forced to use it in the future. It may include, for example, municipalities that, with the establishment of a conservation area, lose the basis for tax revenues. Or it may include the workers in an agroindustry surrounding a reserve who someday may find themselves without work or income for no fault of their own, or of the agroindustry, and who find the reserve the most convenient place to settle down.

Neighbors are not only those who live nearby; they include many sectors of society that may live far from the region in question, but depend on its resources to satisfy actual and future needs: for hydroelectric energy and building materials, for example, or medicines and genes for crop improvement. Often several sectors at a time will have specific mandates from government that influence what goes on in a region. It does not take very long to find out that without such institutions playing an active part in the debate on the region's future, conservation would easily lose. Rather than skirting around these issues, the new regional planning invites the participation of these other user groups. Thus, regional economics maintains its important role but with a twist brought on by the next success of the environmental movement.

4

A broadened development agenda. Broadening the agenda of development by introducing a long list of "new" participants in the development process is a third accomplishment of the environmental movement. This list includes, in our minds at least, the emphasis now given to the physical, social, cultural, and spiritual needs of local populations in general, and of indigenous or other traditionally resident populations in particular. It also includes biodiversity conservation. The list of things to include gets longer as new needs are encountered and as other, older needs gain political support for their solution.

Even with all of these successes, however, some very difficult development problems remain. These problems include formidable land-tenure conflicts and sectoral proposals for large, almost overwhelming, projects of the kind that sweep away everything else in their path. And they include a lack of small viable projects that tend to keep humans healthy and interested and conflicts small and manageable.

Systems thinking. The fourth achievement was to clarify the value of systems thinking in the development process. What this means is that an understanding of the importance of system interactions demands that development planning be integrated. Development, as we have defined it, is always of urgent priority and the strategies formulated through the new regional planning carry along with them a package of projects that fit both the needs of the people and the realities of the place. Such projects must be formulated through a process of integration that will help public and private agencies and interests overcome the problems brought about by their having to live and act in shared systems. For the new regional planning, the process is as important as the product. It incorporates the only sustainable development criteria and standards that have so far been successful: integration, transparency, public participation, and search for consensus.

By its iterative and integrated nature, the new regional planning looks at the needs of those who share the system in question; it understands the limits of the resources available to solve those needs; and it reflects broad agreement over the use of those resources. Thus, in short, the new regional planning looks towards cooperation and coordination, it is integrated and integrative, it is developmental, and, within that category, it is conservationist.

References

Allen, S. 1955. *Conserving Natural Resources: Principles and Practices in a Democracy.* New York. McGraw-Hill.

IUCN/UNEP/WWF. 1980. *World Conservation Strategy: Living Resource Conservation for Sustainable Development.* Gland, Switzerland. International Union for Conservation of Nature and Natural Resources.

McHarg, Ian L. 1971. *Design with Nature.* Garden City, New York. Doubleday.

OEA. 1967a. *Reconocimiento y Evaluación de los Recursos Naturales de la República Dominicana.* Washington, D.C. Secretaría General, Organización de los Estados Americanos.

OEA. 1967b. *El Parque Nacional del Cutibireni: Proyecto Piloto en la Selva del Perú.* Washington, D.C. Secretaría General, Organización de los Estados Americanos.

OAS. 1984. *Integrated Regional Development Planning: Guidelines and Case Studies from OAS Experience.* Washington, D.C. General Secretariat, Organization of American States.

Samuelson, P.S. 1976. *Economics.* 10th ed. New York. McGraw-Hill.

Saunier, R.E. 1992. "People: Key Players in Rain Forest Drama." *Forum for Applied Research and Public Policy*, vol. 7, no. 4. pp. 16-19.

USDA. 1937. *Soil Survey Manual.* Washington, D.C. United States Department of Agriculture. (USDA Misc. Pub. 274)

WCED. 1987. *Our Common Future: The Report of the World Commission on Development and Environment.* World Commission on Environment and Development. New York. Oxford University Press.

6

Chapter 2

IN-SITU CONSERVATION OF BIODIVERSITY

William J. Possiel, Richard E. Saunier,
and Richard A. Meganck

Introduction

The 1992 United Nations Conference on Environment and Development, held in Rio de Janeiro, brought the topic of biodiversity conservation into the living rooms of the world and helped place this critical issue on the agendas of world leaders. While the ranks of those concerned with biodiversity seem to have diversified and increased, a basic understanding of what it is, what it means to mankind, and how it can be protected is still lacking.

In an effort to solve these problems, the World Conservation Union has attempted to clarify the definition and show the value of "biodiversity." Going beyond "genetic makeup," the IUCN interprets biodiversity to encompass all species of plants, animals, and microorganisms and the ecosystems (including ecosystem processes) to which they belong. Usually considered at three different levels--genetic diversity, species diversity, and ecosystem diversity--it is the complicated mosaic of living organisms that interact with abiotic substances and gradients to sustain life at all hierarchical levels (McNeely, 1990). Furthermore, each of these levels extends enormous, often immeasurable, economic and social benefits to mankind. Although it is recognized that a very high percentage of the total biodiversity exists in a small number of tropical countries, significant diversity also occurs in temperate zones and in aquatic ecosystems as well.

Biodiversity conservation is accomplished in a number of ways. *Ex-situ* methods focus on species conservation in botanic gardens, zoos, gene banks, and captive breeding programs. *In-situ* methods use conservation areas as "warehouses" of biological information. Many scientists and conservationists feel that until methods are available to

7

discern easily which of the millions of species and varieties will have economic value, *in-situ* conservation through the protection of natural areas should be the primary means for the maintenance of these resources. However, a rigid preservation approach is virtually impossible to implement and even less likely to be maintained over time. Considering trends in population growth and the urgency of economic development--especially in the developing countries--a more appropriate response would be to pursue proactive alternatives to high-impact development activities, and to implement carefully formulated strategies for *in-situ* methods that would include protected areas in the development mix.

Unfortunately, the formulation of that development mix is not easy, because moral, as well as technical and economic, choices are involved. According to Wilson (1984):

> To choose what is best for the near future is easy. To choose what is best for the distant future is easy. To choose what is best for both the near and distant futures is a hard task, often internally contradictory, and requiring ethical codes yet to be formulated.

Although integrated regional development planning makes no claim to moral superiority, it does provide a framework for making such very difficult choices. That biodiversity conservation must be a part of development planning efforts is clear.

In-Situ Conservation of Biodiversity and Protected Areas

Although viable populations of some organisms can be maintained *ex-situ* either under cultivation or in captivity, these methods are far less effective than *in-situ* methods, and, generally, they are extremely costly. Likewise, although *ex-situ* methods are important under a number of conditions, *in-situ* methods are generally recognized as being more secure and financially efficient. The challenge in using *in-situ* methods is to expand our vision of protected areas to include multiple use and extractive reserves and to develop new models for conservation including, for example, such innovative proposals as using damaged ecosystems to preserve rare, endangered, and threatened species (Cairns,

1986) and to expand the range of options available for economic development.

As of 1993 nearly 7,000 parks and protected areas covering in excess of 650 million acres had been established worldwide (WRI, 1992). When combined with smaller areas such as state parks and private reserves, a large portion of the planet's land surface is receiving some degree of protection. All eight Natural Realms and 14 Biomes, as categorized by Udvardy (1975), are represented. Nevertheless, the participants in the IVth World Congress on National Parks and Protected Areas and the 1992 Earth Summit concluded that although progress had been made in conserving samples of these biogeographic provinces, coverage was still insufficient. Indeed, there is scientific consensus that the total expanse of protected areas needs to be increased by a factor of three in order to maintain the earth's biotic resources (McNeely *et al.*, 1990). Properly conserving these underrepresented provinces will require the establishment of additional areas that are properly funded and managed to ensure that the broadest possible range of biotic resources are protected and available to support future economic development (UNEP, 1992).

Advantages, Risks, and Opportunities

In-situ maintenance of biodiversity through the establishment of conservation and multiple-use areas offers distinct advantages over off-site methods in terms of coverage, viability of the resource, and the economic sustainability of the methods:

(1) *Coverage.* A worldwide system of protected and multiple-use areas would allow a significant number of indigenous species and systems to be protected, thus taking care of the unknowns until such time as methods are found for their investigation and utilization (Burley, 1986).

(2) *Viability.* Natural selection and community evolution continue and new communities, systems, and genetic material are produced (World Conservation Monitoring Center, 1992; Soulé, 1986).

(3) *Economic sustainability.* A country that maintains specific examples of biodiversity stores up future economic benefits. When the need develops and this diversity is thoroughly examined, commercially valuable genetic and biochemical material may be found (Eisner, 1990, 1992, and Reid, 1993).

9

It is not sufficient to establish a conservation area and then assume its biodiversity is automatically protected and without risk. Many risks, both natural and man-created, remain. An extreme example was the near-obliteration of the entire remaining habitat of the golden lion tamarin (*Leontopithecus r. rosalia*) in 1992 by fire (Castro, 1995). Shaffer (1981) cites four broad categories of natural risk:

(1) *Demographic uncertainty* resulting from random events in the survival and reproduction of individuals.

(2) *Environmental uncertainty* due to random, or at least unpredictable, changes in weather, food supply, and the populations of competitors, predators, parasites, etc.

(3) *Natural catastrophes* such as floods, fires, or droughts, which may occur at random intervals.

(4) *Genetic uncertainty* or random changes in genetic make-up due to genetic drift or inbreeding that alter the survival and reproductive probabilities of individuals.

The greatest uncertainties, however, are often anthropogenic. The elimination of habitat to make way for human settlement and associated development activities is the most important factor contributing to the diminishing mosaic of biodiversity. These uncertainties can only be met with a full array of conservation programs, including those that use *ex-situ* methods.

Despite the long list of uncertainties and risk, there is hope for progress. In the last decade not only have pressures from the scientific community and the efforts of non-governmental organizations led to stronger language in international agreements, but segments of the development community have accepted the idea that a large degree of compatibility exists between the need to develop and the need to maintain biodiversity. Further acceptance depends, however, on a number of attitudinal adjustments on the part of many who call for *in-situ* conservation, as well as on a clearer understanding of the rationale behind it by those whose activities conflict with it. The success of conservation also requires a modification of how we cost economic goods and services in the short, medium, and long term (McNeely, 1988).

Globally, the possibilities for undertaking *in-situ* programs such as national parks, biological reserves, and other conservation areas appear to be somewhat favorable. However, the status of these protected areas is often not healthy and unforeseen problems repeatedly arise. The establishment of the Gurupi Biological Reserve in the eastern Brazilian

Amazon, for example, significantly increased the level of threat by causing a rush of illegal extraction of forest resources. This site is probably the most endangered conservation unit in the Amazon basin (Rylands, 1991; Oren, 1988). Worldwide, the list of endangered protected areas is growing in number, and additional human-dominated activities such as water development, mining, road construction and resulting development, livestock grazing, poaching, logging, and other removal of vegetation continue to threaten their integrity (IUCN/UNEP/WWF, 1991).

Integrated Regional Development Planning and Implementation

As is the case with all human activities, alleviating threats to conservation areas requires the involvement of those most affected by the various land-use alternatives in the decision-making process. Integrated regional development planning (IRDP) is a response to the need for better integration of the numerous interests holding conflicting views of how the resources of a region are to be used (Saunier, 1983; OAS, 1984). Support from the conservation community has also been noted (Riklefs *et al.*, 1984):

> The idea of basing conservation of particular species on the maintenance of the natural diversity of species will become even less tenable as the number of threatened species increases and their refuges disappear. Natural areas will have to be designed in conjunction with the goals of regional development and justified on the basis of ecological processes operating within the entire developed region and not just within natural areas.

Not only does IRDP address the intersections between terrestrial, aquatic, and marine systems, it considers the demands of those who use and who would use these systems. However, instead of confronting environmental complexity by subdividing issues into sectoral components, it divides the region into smaller spatial units and looks at the sectoral interactions in each. Interactions of this kind are often conflictive for two reasons: (a) competition is established for the same goods or services by two or more interest groups; and (b) the mix of available goods and services is changed, and one sector is harmed as a result of the activities

11

of another sector to make use of goods and services selected from the whole. IRDP also analyzes the interactions of the region with neighboring areas. Once the regional and sub-regional systems are defined, connections between neighboring units are better understood (Saunier, 1984).

Whereas sectoral planning (including the planning of resource conservation activities) designs programs and projects to meet the needs of specific target populations, IRDP uses methods of systems analysis and conflict management to attempt an appropriate distribution of the costs and benefits of development activities throughout the affected populations or sectors. Thus, conflict identification and its management are fundamental requirements for a development plan to be "integrated" (Saunier, 1984). Sectoral integration is necessary because individual sectoral activities often hinder the activities of other sectors in their efforts to appropriate goods and services from the same and allied systems (Meganck and Saunier, 1983; OAS, 1987). This can be illustrated by agricultural development that affects water quality, resulting in impacts on the goods and services provided by clean water. The decision as to which activities are the correct ones or how each can be adjusted to reduce conflict can only be made through negotiation by the parties involved and not by one of the individual sectors trying to dictate to others--be that sector forestry, agriculture, livestock production, or biodiversity conservation.

In this context, IRDP has a number of advantages over sectoral planning. Conflicts are always easier to manage and even resolve before time, funds, and political prestige have been invested in a specific project. Participants in the regional planning exercise, though representing individual interests, have a shared commitment to rules and procedures of the process that can be controlled. Under this model, the various parties (sectoral interests) operate with a similar rationale and can be easily encouraged to focus on criteria rather than on positions. Further, each can insist that evaluation criteria be objective. This provides an opportunity to invest in options that offer mutual gain and minimal conflict. The result is a strategy for development that demonstrates concern for both the target and the affected populations of development projects and programs, including those that have a conservation orientation. Where integrated analysis and planning show them to be necessary, projects of biodiversity conservation are in all ways development activities, as defensible as any other (Saunier, 1993).

12

To be successful, the recommendations, strategies, and policies that come out of the integrated regional planning process must consider the needs of those affected by linkages between development sectors--which are little more than a reflection of the integrated nature of the ecosystems and landscapes where development takes place (OAS, 1978). Economic interactions are an important part of these systems and landscapes. "The more we overlook the linkages, the more we shall find the sectors fail to function efficiently and productively, with all that implies for sustainable development" (Myers, 1993).

The principles of IRDP, if adapted to the problems of *in-situ* conservation of biodiversity, can provide conservationists with welcome tools. Although much of the effort is based on the agreement of parties, this planning has a scientific foundation, and once it has been clarified and accepted by the planning team, strategic alliances will have been developed for the implementation of the programs. Demonstration projects can then be initiated to help "sell" the strategy or plan. The process then goes forward in a series of iterations of implementation, experimentation, evaluation, and, as needed, modification (Figure 1).

(1) *Scientific information.* Scientific information helps the credibility of the planning process by providing a sound basis for logical decision-making. In more traditional planning efforts, linkages tend to be ignored because our view of the world is traditionally grounded in splitting it up into manageable units. Although science is often responsible for this fragmentation, we also know from science that everything is related, in some way and to some degree, to everything else. That interrelatedness requires that information be managed in an integrated way if we are to make fact-based decisions. "Specialized knowledge by itself produces nothing. It can become productive only when it is integrated into a task" (Drucker, 1994).

Information from the social as well as the natural sciences can help develop a framework for decision-making only if it is both valid and accessible. The collection, storage, and use of relevant information should be designed to provide data rather than assumptions. Thus, one objective of any regional planning effort is to establish a permanent and dynamic database that looks toward addressing information needs on the physical, biotic, and socioeconomic characteristics of the region.

These collections of information should be linked to a larger system of information management to provide complete transparency for all the collaborators. Likewise, if the principal collaborators on the database can help in its design and modification, they will have a sense of ownership in the outcome. Other considerations for designing an information system include the establishment of goals, the determination of the methods and scales to be used, the resolution of the management structure, and the design of evaluation programs.

Figure 1. Principles of Integrated
Regional Development Planning and Implementation

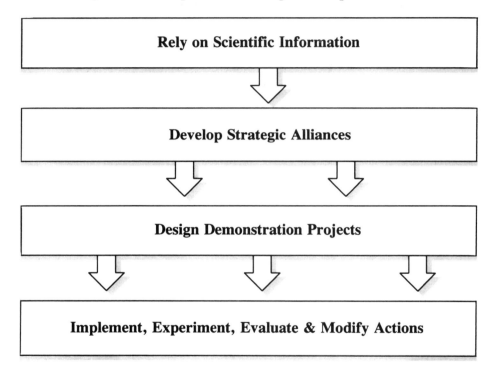

(2) *Develop strategic alliances.* We are often faced with a broad array of development alternatives the selection and implementation of which require the formation of strategic alliances.

To select the best among a number of development alternatives requires the ability to identify costly and undesirable effects of the possible alternative projects and the opportunity to modify these projects during their design stage. Review and discussion in a variety of forums, including those that are cross-sectoral and those where public participation is encouraged, can greatly strengthen planning because of the alliances that are built up in the process.

By making planning a democratic process through IRDP, people can define their problems and design their own solutions. By the same token, IRDP is strengthened through the formation of networks which make use of a variety of communication techniques to assemble knowledgeable and informed constituencies. Four types of networks are valuable to a communication strategy (Krackhardt, 1993):

a. Advice network. Both planning and implementation require an "advice network" of prominent collaborators on whom others depend (or will depend) to solve problems and provide technical information concerning the strategy, program, or project being developed.

b. Trust network. A "trust network" consists of the inner circle of participants who share sensitive political information and back each other in a crisis. These are often the project initiators, who may act as catalysts to help in conflict management or to ensure project implementation through their leadership.

c. Communication network. Participants in the effort should discuss project-related matters regularly. Such a network can be specifically designed to inform politically important individuals on a timely basis, thus ensuring their feedback and support.

d. Constituent network. The need to form an alliance with a number of diverse constituencies often takes the planner into the realm of the unknown. Part of communication is recognizing that we can learn from others. An exchange of ideas is important and at least four approaches can be used to foster this exchange, including information feedback, consultation, joint planning, and delegated authority (Westman, 1985). Information feedback consists of formal and informal one-way presentations, newspaper articles, notices, etc. Consultations are made through such mechanisms as public hearings, ombudspersons, or representatives of the interest groups concerned. Joint planning can take place through the use of advisory committees, structured workshops, etc. And delegated authority is amenable to the use of citizens' review boards and planning commissions.

(3) *Design demonstration projects.* The value of an interdisciplinary and multifunctional planning team cannot be overstated; alliances forged in the process are indispensable to the success of the decisions that are taken. Innovative demonstration projects must include cross-sectoral representation from the initial stages of their formulation. The design of both the planning process and its products should have clear goals and objectives, review existing legislation and public policy, assess the social and economic conditions of the region, describe important ecosystem structure and function, and analyze direct and indirect threats to both the process and its products (Figure 2).

Figure 2. How to Design Demonstration Projects

16

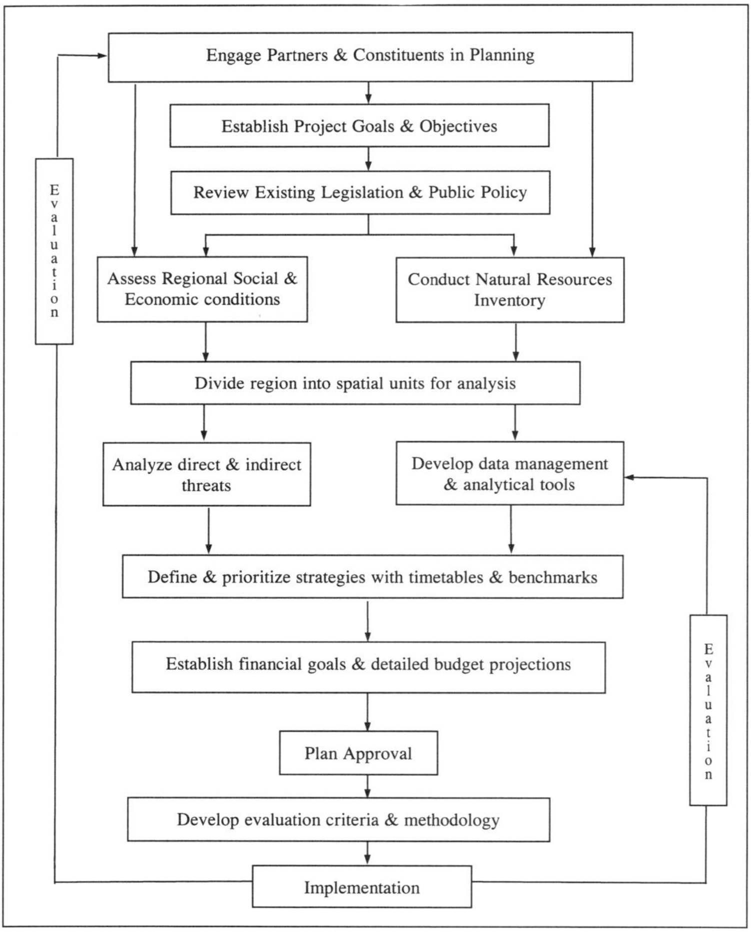

All of this is more easily done if the region is divided into smaller homogeneous units for analysis and if partnerships are created from the variety of constituencies. A series of strategies, with timetables and benchmarks, should be established with detailed financial goals and budget projections. Visual and graphic tools can be used successfully to communicate the process and products to those who require timely information for decision-making. The successful plan also contains criteria and methods for evaluating progress towards meeting the established goals.

(4) *Implement, experiment, evaluate and modify actions.* The goal of any planning process is its implementation. Countless development plans that have never been implemented sit on shelves because of problems with funding, politics, myopic vision, or the lack of qualified personnel to take the planning recommendations and make them a reality. In many government settings, the fear of being associated with a project or program that is connected to a current or previous administration can be risky. Developing communication strategies to transfer knowledge to decision-makers can ameliorate this fear.

The implementation of a plan requires that strategies and specific actions be prioritized and that public policy be formulated to do so. Accountability must be maintained, but those who are charged with the implementation of a program must recognize that there are productive failures and that implementation can be modified in positive ways either because of such failures or because of experimentation.

Conclusion

There are no easy solutions to the complex challenges of integrated regional development planning. A process which provides a thoughtful structure for gathering and utilizing scientific information, which involves stakeholders in a genuine analysis of development alternatives, and which establishes clear and measurable objectives can provide for rational development activities, including those for the conservation of biodiversity. Using IRDP as a vehicle to communicate with decision-makers provides a framework for action. Planners often look for what is politically expedient; however, the participation of non-governmental organizations can play an extremely important role in tempering politically motivated development. This nexus between

17

government and non-governmental organizations is one of the more important areas where "integrated" regional development takes place. Both should represent the interests of both present and future generations.

References

Bibby, C.J. *et al.* (eds.). 1992. *Putting Biodiversity on the Map: Priority Areas for Global Conservation.* Cambridge, U.K. International Council for Bird Preservation.

Burley, F. William. 1988. "Monitoring Biological Diversity for Setting Priorities in Conservation." In E.O. Wilson (ed.), *Biodiversity.* Washington, D.C. National Academy Press. pp. 227-230.

Cairns, J. Jr. 1987. "Disturbed Ecosystems as Opportunities for Research in Restoration Ecology." In William Jordan *et al.* (eds.), *Restoration Ecology: A Synthetic Approach to Ecological Research.* New York. Cambridge University Press. pp. 307-319.

Castro, Inés. 1995. Smithsonian Institution. Personal communication.

Drucker, Peter F. 1994. "The Theory of Business." *Harvard Business Review*, vol. 72, no. 5. pp. 95-104.

Eisner, Thomas. 1990. "Prospecting for Nature's Chemical Riches." *Issues in Science and Technology.* vol. 6. pp. 31-34.

Eisner, Thomas. 1992. "Chemical Prospecting: A Proposal for Action." In F.H. Bormann and S.R. Kellert (eds.), *Ecology, Economics, and Ethics: The Broken Circle.* New Haven. Yale University Press. pp. 196-202.

IUCN/UNEP/WWF. 1991. *Caring for the Earth: A Strategy for Sustainable Living.* Gland, Switzerland. World Conservation Union.

Krackhardt, David, and Jeffrey R. Hanson. 1993. "Informal Networks: The Company Behind the Chart." *Harvard Business Review*, vol. 71, no. 4. pp. 104-111.

McNeely, J.A. 1988. "Values and Benefits of Biological Diversity." In J. A. McNeely (ed.), *Economics and Biological Diversity.* Gland, Switzerland. International Union for the Conservation of Nature and Natural Resources. pp. 9-36.

McNeely, J.A., *et. al.* 1990. *Conserving the World's Biological Diversity.* Gland, Switzerland, and Washington, D.C. World Conservation Union and World Resources Institute.

Meganck, R.A., and R.E. Saunier. 1983. "What Trinidad and Tobago Must Know about Managing Our Natural Resources." *The Naturalist,* vol. 4, no. 8.

Myers, Norman. 1993. "The Question of Linkages in Environment and Development: We Can No Longer Afford to Split the World into Disciplinary Components." *BioScience,* vol. 43, no. 5. pp. 302-310.

OAS. 1978. *Environmental Quality and River Basin Development: A Model for Integrated Analysis and Planning.* Washington, D.C. General Secretariat, Organization of American States.

OAS. 1984. *Integrated Development Planning: Guidelines and Case Studies from OAS Experience.* Washington, D.C. General Secretariat, Organization of American States.

OAS. 1987. *Minimum Conflict: Guidelines for Planning the Development of American Humid Tropical Environments.* Washington, D.C. General Secretariat, Organization of American States.

Oren, David C. 1988. "Uma Reserva Biológica para o Maranhão." *Ciencia Hoje,* vol. 8, no. 44. pp. 37-45.

Reid, Walter V., *et al.* 1993. *Biodiversity Prospecting: Using Genetic Resources for Sustainable Development.* Washington, D.C. World Resources Institute.

Riklefs, R.E., Z. Naveh, and R.E. Turner. 1984. *Conservation of Ecological Processes.* Gland, Switzerland. International Union for the Conservation of Nature and Natural Resources. (Commission on Ecology Paper 8)

Rylands, A.B. 1991. *The Status of Conservation Areas in the Brazilian Amazon.* Washington, D.C. World Wildlife Fund.

Saunier, Richard E. 1983. "A Future Together?" *Development Forum,* vol. XI, no. 8, Nov-Dec.

Saunier, Richard E. 1984. "Regional Approaches Utilized in Development Planning." *Natural Resource Technical Bulletin,* no. 5. (AID-NPS Natural Resources Project)

Saunier, Richard E. 1993. "The Place of Tourism in Island Ecosystems." Paper presented to the Regional Conference on Health and Sustainable Tourism Development (Nassau, Bahamas, 9-11 Nov. 1993).

Shaffer, M.L. 1981. "Minimum Population Sizes for Species Conservation." *BioScience*, vol. 31, no. 30. pp. 131-134.

Soulé, Michael E. 1986. *Conservation Biology: The Science of Scarcity and Diversity*. Sunderland, Mass. Sinauer Assoc.

Udvardy, M.D.F. 1975. *A Classification of the Biogeographical Provinces of the World*. Morges, Switzerland. International Union for the Conservation of Nature. (IUCN Occasional Paper No. 18)

Westman, Walter E. 1985. *Ecology, Impact Assessment, and Environmental Planning*. New York. John Wiley & Sons.

Wilson, E.O. 1984. *Biophilia*. Cambridge, Mass. Harvard University Press.

WRI/UNEP/UNDP. 1992. *World Resources 1992-93*. New York. Oxford University Press.

Chapter 3

BIODIVERSITY CONSERVATION AND TRADITIONAL AGROECOSYSTEMS

Jeffrey A. McNeely

Introduction

For rural people, wild plants and animals provide food, medicine, building materials, income, and a source of inspiration. Rivers and lakes give them transportation, water, and fish; and the coastal zone offers them a permanent source of sustenance and building materials. But instead of a sustainable flow of renewable resources, mostly furnished by nature, recent patterns of agricultural development are depleting soils and genetic and species diversity both in the cropped areas and in the surrounding ecosystems.

Agricultural lands, livestock grazing areas, manipulated forests, and other human-managed ecosystems cover at least two-thirds of the terrestrial surface of the planet, whereas protected areas cover only about 8 percent (McNeely *et al.*, 1994). The remaining percentage is wilderness, urban lands, etc. These human-managed ecosystems contain an important segment of global biodiversity, and if they are managed with this in mind--especially if they are managed in conjunction with a system of protected areas--they can significantly contribute to the maintenance of global biodiversity.

Since the beginning of this century alone, about 75 percent of the genetic diversity of the most important crops has disappeared from farmers' fields (Cary and Mooney, 1990). This has increased agricultural vulnerability and reduced the essential variety of the diets of rural people. Other traditional and local species and races of domesticated plants and animals, vital for the nutrition of the poorest people, are underutilized or neglected. In fisheries and aquaculture, the introduction and transfer of exotic organisms has helped local economies but sometimes at the expense of natural systems, cultural stability, and social equity. The symmetry between the development of rural areas and the conservation of many forms of established land use is a critical issue that regional planning needs to address if biodiversity is to be maintained in the long term.

Agriculture and the Conservation of Biodiversity

Each agricultural village is part of an ecosystem. These agricultural ecosystems vary widely--from broad expanses of river deltas with the possibility of year-round irrigation, to areas of seasonally irrigated fields interspersed among forests, to areas dominated by rain-fed crops. Legumes, cereals, tubers, herbs, fruits, trees, livestock, wild animals, and fish all play important roles in most agricultural villages and must therefore be considered in planning agricultural development projects. Further, the relationships of each agricultural community extend far beyond the village itself, and these must be considered also. For example, in the hills of Nepal, each hectare of farmland needs the support of 3.48 hectares of forest and these forests require expert management if they are to continue to provide benefits in terms of food, fodder, firewood, construction materials, medicines, water, clothing, etc.

Agricultural systems will change dramatically over the coming decades because of climate change, new technologies based on genetic engineering and agroecology, and shifts in international markets. Governments and farmers will need to adapt to these changes through planning. Indicative planning, for example, is a system of dynamic planning informed by, and constantly adjusting to, changes in leading indicators. These indicators could be modified to include those related to agriculture and biodiversity in order to help ensure that agricultural systems will robustly resist mere transitory changes. In conjunction with ongoing efforts to develop environmental accounting systems, research should be initiated to find the most effective indicators and monitoring systems (Ahmad *et al.*, 1989).

Traditional agriculture can contribute to easing the stress of changing conditions in rural areas, help conserve biodiversity, and maintain healthy relationships between rural people and the land. For example, in traditional systems of shifting cultivation, or swidden agriculture, a wide range of crops--often over 100 at one time--can be grown, essentially transforming a natural forest to one that is cultured.

22

The species and varieties grown in the swiddens are in a state of continuous adaptation, and in many places the crops are enriched by gene exchange with wild or weedy relatives. Altieri and Merrick (1987) contend that "maintenance of traditional agroecosystems is the only sensible strategy to preserve *in-situ* repositories of crop germplasm."

Traditional agriculture has adapted to a wide variety of local conditions, produced a diverse and reliable food supply, reduced the incidence of disease and insect problems, used labor efficiently, intensified production with limited resources, and earned maximum returns with low levels of technology. It makes use of a wide range of species and land races that vary in their reaction to diseases and insect pests, as well as to different conditions of soil, rainfall, and sunlight. Traditional agriculture provides sustainable yields by drawing on centuries of accumulated experience by farmers who have not depended on scientific information, external inputs, capital, credit, or markets.

But with growing populations, steps need to be taken to enhance the productivity of lands under traditional agriculture. In the forested uplands, modern agricultural development should take existing traditional systems as starting points and use modern agricultural science to improve on their productivity. The essential element is to design self-sustaining agroecosystems that assure the maintenance of the local genetic diversity available to farmers, thereby enabling rural communities to maintain control over their production systems. In addition, the maintenance of a stable, permanent link with forested land, such as that contained in some categories of protected areas, enables farmers to invest time and effort in other assets like fruit trees, fenced gardens, terraces, and irrigation canals. Such mixed systems will often make possible a marriage of modern and traditional agricultural techniques leading to the establishment of more permanent villages (McNeely, 1989).

Agricultural ecologists and modern land-use planners have learned to respect the wisdom inherent in much traditional practice. If it is seen as part of an overall system of conservation-oriented management, traditional farming can continue to be a meaningful part of the total agricultural productivity of a region and to contribute to the conservation of its biodiversity.

Planners should also be aware that strict protection does not always lead to more biodiversity. Nabhan *et al.* (1982), studying two oases in the Sonoran Desert on either side of the Mexico-United States border, found that the customary land-use practices of Papago farmers on

23

the Mexican side of the border contributed to the biodiversity of the oasis but that the protection of an oasis 54 km to the northwest, within the U.S. Organpipe Cactus National Monument, resulted in a decline in species diversity over a 25-year period.

On the other hand, some conservation measures can help preserve traditional agroecosystems. The 2,000-ha Rock Coral Canyon Reserve, for example, which is owned by the U.S. Department of Agriculture and is one of just a handful of places in North America where wild varieties of chili peppers grow naturally, is the focus of the first proposed government-sponsored *in-situ* conservation plan for wild native crops. The project is run by Native Seeds/SEARCH, an NGO that aims to preserve and exploit some of the wild edible species in the region. It is estimated that colonizers since Columbus have wiped out two-thirds of North America's native crop varieties (Chatterjee, 1992). Apart from peppers, the reserve is home to four other important wild varieties of native crops: tepary beans, cotton, squashes, and *Agave* sp., from which tequila is made. These species have traditionally been gathered by the local Tohono O'Odham people. As recently as 70 years ago, the Tohono O'Odham cultivated 4,000 ha of farms in Arizona without having to pump ground water--an impossible dream for most farms in the state today. Eating tepary and lima beans, pods from mesquite trees, acorns, and corn, they had an extremely healthful diet.

Threats to Traditional Agroecosystems

Modern farming technology is now removing innovation from the farm and placing it instead in the laboratory. The uniform varieties produced at the research center, with their dependence on chemical fertilizers and pesticides, are displacing farm-bred varieties. Once these traditional varieties are gone, the knowledge of their cultivation and use is also lost.

But neither is the "museum" approach to conservation sufficient. Fencing off ecosystems valued for their diversity as protected areas, keeping plants in botanic gardens, and storing germ plasm in seed banks is hardly an adaptive long-term solution. It seems apparent that preserving genetic variety is pointless unless the farming system that produced it is also preserved, along with its climate and soil and the accumulated knowledge of its cultivation and use.

But traditional agroecosystems are under threat in virtually all parts of the world. Above all, these threats come from agricultural policies that favor centralized control and the subsidies required to achieve them. While these policies have undoubtedly increased total agricultural productivity, they have also led to considerable economic inefficiencies and vulnerabilities. The solutions are to be found in correcting inappropriate agricultural policies, including those that guide land-use planning.

Despite impressive increases in agricultural productivity in recent decades, many current agricultural policies are economically inefficient and environmentally unsound. They benefit farmers with large landholdings growing few crops and penalize farmers with smaller holdings that often cultivate many crops. Food price controls and subsidies for agricultural inputs help meet short-term consumer demands but remove incentives for increased agricultural production, and they often tend to undermine food security. Such policies have also decreased the diversity of species used by farmers, increased the uniformity of crops and livestock breeds, and made farmers dependent on expensive and often unreliable sources of agricultural inputs. Although many agronomists argue that uniformity in agricultural practices can improve productivity, the Global Biodiversity Strategy (WRI/IUCN/UNEP, 1992) points out five current policies that are likely to be contrary to the interests of long-term agricultural productivity:

(1) *Agricultural input subsidies.* Reducing the cost of inputs such as water, pesticides, and chemical fertilizers leads to the promotion of "industrial" agriculture based on a small number of highly uniform crops at the expense of farming systems based on a wider variety of crops. Subsidized inputs sometimes also replace natural processes based on biodiversity that are equally effective at lower cost to people and have less impact on the supporting ecosystems. The growing use of pesticides, for example, has displaced natural enemies of agricultural pests such as micro-organisms and invertebrates.

(2) *Food price subsidies.* Policies to reduce food prices for urban consumers can cut into farm profits. Combined with subsidies for inputs, such price controls can greatly reduce agricultural diversity. The use of modern crop varieties, which require irrigation and heavy inputs of agrochemicals, can enable some farmers to neutralize the impact of food price controls. But farmers using low-input systems and traditional varieties receive no such offsetting benefit, which discourages them from

developing new varieties of their own; this leads indirectly to the erosion of knowledge of traditional varieties.

(3) *Overvalued exchange rates.* Many governments of developing countries have overvalued their currencies as a means of subsidizing imported capital goods for industry, reducing the costs of imported food, and lowering the price of food for export. Basically, such policies "tax" all agriculture, but farmers who use fewer manufactured inputs are taxed relatively more than those who use more of these inputs. Like the combination of subsidies and food price controls discussed above, this combination favors industrial agriculture with its attendant reduction in biodiversity.

(4) *Research biased toward high-input agriculture.* Much national agricultural research has been directed toward increasing the production of a few major crops through technology change. This research model has been exported from the industrialized to the developing world through the Consultative Group on International Agricultural Research (CGIAR), and may have provided much-needed breathing room in the race between production and population. But to meet future production needs, national governments must support agricultural systems that meet food needs while maintaining important components of diversity.

(5) *Credit policies* that discriminate against "minor" crops and traditional varieties. All too often, governments fail to extend agricultural credit to farmers planting traditional crop varieties or growing crops consumed locally. Particularly in developing countries, where the benefits of "improved" varieties may be negligible in marginal agriculture, reduced productivity and accelerated loss of crop diversity may result.

Traditional agriculture is now also threatened by the new global consumer culture, which is spreading through television, trade, and other means. Management systems that were effective for thousands of years have become obsolete in a few decades, replaced by systems of exploitation that bring short-term profits for a few and long-term costs for many. A few examples will indicate the range of factors driving this process.

Land-use management throughout much of sub-Saharan Africa is evolving from a pre-colonial communal system to systems that are more formal and individualistic. Most traditional communities do not have effective title to or control over their lands, nor do they have an effective way to make their views felt at the national policy level. As a consequence, the colonial period was marked by a taking of many of the most desirable lands from long-term resident communities, and the post-colonial period of nationhood has further served to provide legal vehicles for a taking of land and resources from local communities in the national interest. Added to this are the population pressures on the land that contribute to a breakdown of traditional methods of control. For the Shona of Zimbabwe this scenario of land divestiture has been all too evident. Traditionally, the Shona managed their lands communally on the basis of ancestral relationships. Sacred sites and sites of historical importance were preserved throughout the Shona domain, though outsiders were generally unaware of these areas or of the values attached to them. Consequently, the breakup of Shona lands into small parcels under individual ownership schemes failed to maintain traditional land protection and management systems, and resulted in a loss of cultural heritage and its associated sustainable farming practices (IUCN, 1993).

Robinson (1993) describes how colonists have been moving into the territory of the Yuqui Indians in Peru, primarily for the purpose of producing coca. These colonists tend to remain on their farms only during coca planting and harvesting, and return to their highland settlements at other times of the year. Their activities appear to have had a major impact on the fish and game available to the Yuqui because they use technology (such as fishing with dynamite) that leads to considerable overexploitation of resources. This is just one of many examples that could be provided of how new colonists have moved into traditional lands and disrupted the traditional systems that had worked over a period of many generations. Crosby (1987) describes the impacts Europeans have had on both cultures and ecosystems during the thousand years of their "ecological imperialism."

In the Moluccas of eastern Indonesia, rapidly rising consumer desires, stimulated by television images and the objects of a growing Indonesian middle class, are pushing local governments and officials to shorten the interval between traditionally controlled fish harvests (Zerner, 1993). The rationale is that the increased population densities on isolated islands lead to further needs for alternative sources of income. Despite evidence that shortened intervals result in drastically decreased stocks of marine resources, local government officials claim that the needs of villagers for income--to conduct religious rituals, pay school fees, or acquire consumer goods--are forcing them to extend the period of harvest.

Hunting has long been an important part of the economy on the island of Sumbawa, in the eastern part of the Indonesian archipelago. Because most of the villagers are Muslims, pigs are not a particularly desirable game animal, but feral buffalo and cattle, as well as the local species of deer, *Cervus timorensis*, are commonly hunted. As grazers, these species do far better in grasslands than in the forest--the normal vegetative cover of the island. Today, however, grassland covers 17 percent of Sumbawa's land area. These grasslands are several hundred years old and have always been used for grazing and hunting. The grasslands are maintained by annual fires which, while preventing reforestation, replace older and less palatable grasses with younger and more edible ones, eliminate dead plant material, and actually increase overall herbaceous productivity. The creation of grasslands by these villagers is sensible habitat management that creates conditions favoring the grazing animals at the expense of pigs (which prefer the forest). Furthermore, the replacement of forest by grassland has been of net benefit to the wild herbivores that are hunted, with populations kept at such a high level that they could be harvested virtually at will. The hunters accept communal control that proscribes hunting during the period from November to May when the deer give birth and rear their young. Government conservation programs prohibit both the burning of the savannas and the hunting of the main game animals--excluding wild pigs, the only species the Islamic islanders avoided. Because of this insensitivity to the local reality, a genuine symbiosis that had proved sustainable over long periods of time was broken, the acceptance of the program by peasant hunters was lost, and their traditional conservation measures were undermined (Dove, 1984). The process has led to the loss of both biological and cultural diversity.

Tenure: The Key Issue

A key concern for planners is the traditional links between indigenous cultures and the natural world; it deals with the responsibility over resources. Tenure systems upon which responsibility is built are based on legitimacy drawn from the community in which they operate rather than from the nation-state in which they are located (Lynche and Alcorn, 1993). Indigenous systems of resource tenure are extremely variable, complex mixtures of individual and community rights, enforced by the local culture. These systems are flexible and constantly evolving, often in response to changing environmental conditions. Such systems invariably are being disrupted by nation-states claiming ownership of the most important areas.

The institutional control of resources by local peoples tends to be strongest when the groups are the most independent. Once they become integrated into larger systems, the social and economic center of gravity shifts away from the community and rural institutions become increasingly marginalized politically (Murphree, 1993).

Local people need the rights to self-determination, and to set their own development agenda. Although this does not guarantee success, it does put responsibility firmly in the hands of those who will earn the benefits and pay the costs. We might reasonably expect that communities will behave in their enlightened self-interest, if empowered to do so.

Security of tenure offers opportunities for communities to gain benefits from their resources, but at least some market forces typically exist exclusively outside local communities. Therefore, resources are perceived differently at national and community levels, and the benefits are derived differently. As a result, governments should consider returning at least some nationalized resource systems, such as forests and wildlife, to community-based tenure systems, which are often more cost-effective. Putting resource management back in the hands of local communities also helps governments divest themselves of responsibility for functions they cannot adequately fulfill. The legitimacy of community-based tenure systems can be recognized through cadastral surveys, assessments of wildlife populations, demarcation, registration, and community infrastructure that can defend against outside pressure.

The full implications of such an "indigenous privatization scheme" need to be considered. Transferring the control of access rights from a national to a local authority puts power into the hands of those making the local decisions. As Murphree (1993) points out, the way that natural resources are used in any particular place and time is the result of conflicting interests between groups of people having different objectives. Seldom does any one group dominate, and resources can be used in a number of different ways at the same time and place. So the variation in resource management is part of an ongoing process in which the different interests and struggles of the various actors are located. Some local actors are likely to benefit more than others, thereby creating new tensions in the community.

It is clear to all farmers living in such systems, says Rappaport (1972), "that their survival is contingent upon the maintenance, rather than the mere exploitation, of the larger community of which they know themselves to be only parts." Regional plans that incorporate means of protecting the larger ecosystem within which agricultural communities survive and flourish are far more likely to succeed than those that are too narrowly based. Such considerations will often involve ensuring that the relevant communities are given management responsibility for the natural areas upon which their continued prosperity depends. Governments should therefore use regional planning as a means to promote closer collaboration between the supporters of agriculture and the supporters of protected areas, building on the common interest in maintaining the diversity and productivity of biotic resources.

References

Ahmad, Y., S. El Sarafy, and Ernst Lutz (eds). 1989. *Environmental Accounting and Sustainable Development*. Washington, D.C. World Bank. (World Bank Symposia Series)

Altieri, M.A., and Laura C. Merrick. 1987. "*In-situ* Conservation of Crop Genetic Resources Through Maintenance of Traditional Farming Systems." *Economic Botany*, vol. 41, no. 1. pp. 86-96.

Chatterjee, Pratap. 1992. "Raising Arizona's Wild Crops." *New Scientist*, 26 Sept. pp. 12, 13.

Crosby, Alfred W. 1987. *Ecological Imperialism: The Biological Expansion of Europe 900-1900*. Cambridge, U.K. Cambridge University Press.

Dove, Michael R. 1984. "Man, Land and Game in Sumbawa: Some Observations on Agrarian Ecology and Development Policy in Eastern Indonesia." *Singapore Journal of Tropical Geography*, vol. 5, no. 2. pp. 112-124.

Fowler, Cary, and Pat Mooney. 1990. *Shattering: Food, Politics, and the Loss of Genetic Diversity*. Tucson. University of Arizona Press.

IUCN. 1993. *Indigenous Peoples and Strategies for Sustainability*. Summary of a Workshop on Strategies for Sustainability (Gland, Switzerland, 31 March-2 April, 1993).

Lynche, Owen J., and Janice B. Alcorn. 1993. "Tenurial Rights and Community-Based Conservation." Paper presented to the Liz Claiborne/Art Ortenburg Foundation Workshop on Community-Based Conservation (Airlie, Virginia, Oct. 18-22).

McNeely, Jeffrey A. 1989. "Conserving Genetic Resources at the Farm Level." *ILEIA Newsletter*, Dec. p. 36.

McNeely, J.A., J. Harrison, and P. Dingwall (eds). 1994. *Protecting Nature: Regional Reviews of Protected Areas.* Gland, Switzerland. World Conservation Union.

Murphree, Marshall W. 1993. "The Role of Institutions." Paper presented to the Liz Claiborne/Art Ortenburg Foundation Workshop on Community-Based Conservation (Airlie, Virginia, Oct. 18-22).

Nabhan, G.P., *et al.* 1982. "Papago Influences on Habitat and Biotic Diversity: Quitovac Oasis EthnoEcology." *Journal of Ethnobiology*, vol. 2, no. 1. pp. 124-143.

Rappaport, Roy A. 1972. "Forests and Man." *Ecologist*, vol. 6, no. 7. pp. 240-246.

Robinson, John G. 1993. "Community-Based Approaches to Wildlife Conservation in Neotropical Forests." Paper presented to the Liz Claiborne/Art Ortenburg Foundation Workshop on Community-Based Conservation (Airlie, Virginia, Oct. 18-22).

WRI/IUCN/UNEP. 1992. *Global Biodiversity Strategy.* Washington, D.C. World Resources Institute.

Zerner, Charles. 1993. "Imaging Marine Resource Management Institutions in the Maluku Islands, Indonesia, 1870-1992." Paper presented to the Liz Claiborne/Art Ortenburg Foundation Workshop on Community-Based Conservation (Airlie, Virginia, Oct. 18-22).

Chapter 4

THE NEED AND POTENTIAL FOR PRIVATE BIODIVERSITY CONSERVATION

Joshua C. Dickinson III

Introduction

I offer here some thoughts on terrestrial and aquatic biodiversity conservation *outside* of parks, in places where biodiversity is not a primary or often even a conscious concern. The pre-eminent threat to biodiversity is seen to be the conversion of natural ecosystems to crops or to grazing land for domestic livestock, or changes initiated with the building of human-made infrastructure. Emphasis is given to private initiatives that result incidentally or purposely in the maintenance of a measure of biodiversity, and to the role of government in guiding and encouraging land use that results in biodiversity conservation. This emphasis is not meant to denigrate the role of and need for parks and reserves located strategically to preserve key ecosystems and important species assemblages. However, because of the limited capacity of governments to achieve a desirable level and extent of protection, a broader approach is needed. It appears prudent to focus more efforts on the 90 percent of the earth's land area that is either in private hands or in public ownership but exploited by private interests.

Important representatives of terrestrial biota exist in all ecosystems, but more attention is given here to forested tropical ecosystems where human pressure appears to be highest. The Holdridge life-zone system is offered as an organizing framework for establishing biodiversity conservation strategies, particularly at the national and regional levels. Land-capability assessment is introduced as a means of justifying the protection of areas with severe biophysical limitations. Marine biodiversity concerns are focused on the diverse estuarine and near-shore marine ecosystems most threatened by human exploitation and settlements.

33

A Basic Assumption

It is a critical assumption that maintaining a diverse array of species and their habitats has value to society. It is also assumed that publicly and privately held natural areas outside of parks must produce goods and services of value to society competitively with alternative uses that usually result in major loses of biodiversity. Where natural-area use is not fully competitive with conversion to other uses, we can assume that society is willing to promote resource use that results in the maintenance of biodiversity by (a) restricting concessional use of public lands, (b) subsidizing non-competitive private uses, or (c) becoming more clever in attributing economic value to ecosystem services, such as flood control, that incidentally result in biodiversity maintenance. Anything short of subsidized preservation (de facto parks) involves some sacrifice of biodiversity.

While life exists everywhere on the planet, the diversity of life happens to be greatest in the developing countries and it is also there that threats to diversity are most intractable. This paper is focused on the logic that peoples who threaten biodiversity through over-consumption require less immediate attention than those who deforest, burn, and overgraze in order to survive.

Multiple Faces of Biodiversity

At the interface of natural science and society's concern for nature, ambiguities and differing perceptions are inevitable. Even among scientists biodiversity conservation has generated controversy, over time and today. Aldo Leopold (1949) believed that the habitat needs of large carnivores should govern efforts to maintain biodiversity: carnivores must be present "to preserve the integrity, stability, and beauty of the biotic community." Although serious efforts continue to maintain megafauna populations, a broader multispecies perspective has evolved. Four of the comparisons that both scientists and planners of resource use address are successional (including weeds) versus climax associations, various small areas versus a few large areas, species-rich versus depauperate systems, and umbrella species (large carnivores) versus overall system diversity (Shafer, 1995). With severe budget limitations choices must be made. The distribution of species that are actually or potentially useful, endangered, scientifically interesting, or beautiful is difficult to predict. The preservation of as large a variety of ecosystems within a particular country as possible appears to be a viable target.

Biodiversity is the total number of species and the distribution of a particular species calculated using formulae to index different attributes of diversity in a specific ecosystem (Odum, 1975). Conservation can be defined as managed resource use that maintains the capacity of natural habitats and agricultural land to produce crops, livestock, timber, fish, or wildlife. Biodiversity could be added to the list of "products" of managed resource use, though a bit awkwardly. Maintaining biodiversity may be either a management objective in itself or a condition on other resource uses, such as timber production. Biodiversity can be an important yardstick of the relative success of our conservation efforts if the formal methods of measuring it are employed consistently over time in accordance with an appropriate sampling regime.

The conservation community must look carefully at what is meant by "biodiversity conservation." Public interest in the subject is sparked by the educational and fund-raising activities of conservation groups that focus on preserving rain forests and certain symbolic vertebrates. The geographic distribution of those concerned about diversity is not uniform and interest increases exponentially with the distance from where it is greatest and most threatened and peaks in places like Washington, D.C., and London. E.O. Wilson's excellent volume *Biodiversity* (1986) contains 57 chapters of which only two were written by experts from tropical countries. Those most knowledgeable and concerned about the importance of maintaining biodiversity also have their basic human needs well met, while those whose daily actions most drastically affect biodiversity do not. If we do not approach biodiversity maintenance through a process that also improves the economic and social well-being of rural people, the effort will most certainly fail. The small cadre of people who can effectively argue the case for biodiversity have to reach out and convince leaders in developing countries, their own national decision-makers, and the unconvinced experts in development agencies.

Why We Are Losing Biodiversity

Failure to value and protect natural ecosystems (read "biodiversity") is driven by deeply rooted cultural preference for disturbed landscapes, real or perceived necessity, and a lack of education of the public and decision-makers. Cultural values are reflected in poor and rich countries alike where subsidies tend to favor the conversion of natural ecosystems to provide for agriculture and pasture--regardless of the value of the goods and services offered by natural ecosystems that are lost. For example, in the United States subsidized grazing replaces poverty as an incentive to disturb arid areas and artificially low stumpage fees in publicly owned forests promotes their mismanagement.

Education on two fronts is needed to reverse the pressure on natural ecosystems. One emphasizes economic evaluation of the goods and services offered by ecosystems, including both known marketable products and services (such as watershed protection) and future benefits yet undiscovered (new crops and medicines). The second is an ethical consideration which stresses that protecting nature is good and prudent, and that the loss of any species is bad. Scientists advocate preserving ecosystems because they contain unique and interesting information.

Both poverty and affluence take their toll on ecosystems and their associated species. However, without a measure of affluence, the loss of ecosystems and species will continue. Affluence provides the opportunity for choice on how ecosystems are to be used, rehabilitated and preserved. Running counter to the human drive to simplify is a love of life that also exists. But without education to enhance and focus innate human *"biophilia"* (Wilson, 1984) into a moral and political force, increased income can increase destructiveness. In the Philippines, for example, increased affluence allows the dynamite fishermen to purchase larger boats and blow away more distant coral reefs.

An Evolving Strategy

For millennia simplification of ecosystems has been our most effective means of assuring that we can direct the sun's energy, water, and nutrients to meet our own needs for food and fiber:

> This was my curious labor all summer--to make this portion of the earth's surface, which had yielded only cinquefoil, blackberries, johnswort and the like, before; sweet wild fruits and pleasant flowers, produce instead this pulse.
>
> ("The Bean-field," from Thoreau's *Walden)*

To persuade the great majority of the world's people to maintain biodiversity in apparent contradiction of their best interests is a formidable challenge. Efforts to date by dedicated conservationists have met surprising success, given the esoteric nature of the theme. The goal of the World Conservation Strategy (IUCN/UNEP/WWF, 1980) has been modest--setting aside 10 percent of each country in national parks and equivalent reserves. Success in this effort has absorbed much of the energy and funds of the conservation community. David Western (cited in Baskin, 1994) points out that past efforts to conserve animal populations in Kenya's parks have been remarkably effective, but that 75 percent of the wildlife is found outside the park boundaries. Probably an even higher percentage of the rain-forest species in the Congo Basin are found outside of parks. The USAID-funded Biodiversity Support Program has established a commission made up predominantly of African professionals to develop a biodiversity-conservation agenda. Because of the African view of parks as a colonial legacy, they avoid linking biodiversity solely to parks, but advocate its conservation wherever it occurs--on farms, in parks, in hedgerows, etc. (BSP, 1993). This approach closely parallels that advocated by Western. In Southern Africa, Zimbabwe is privatizing wildlife management under the CAMPFIRE project (Metcalfe, this volume). But we have to be careful in extrapolating from opportunities for the conservation of wildlife in East and Southern Africa: they have the highly visible "big game" species that people will travel halfway around the world to see or shoot.

Biodiversity in a Life-Zone Context

The IUCN interprets biodiversity to encompass all species of plants, animals, and micro-organisms and the ecosystems (including ecosystem processes) to which they belong. To be useful, this global perspective must be brought to a level, where public awareness and policies must eventually drive actions to maintain biodiversity. We have not identified all species, know little of the value of those we have catalogued, and even less about how to assure their survival. Given this reality, maintaining at least patches of as many ecosystems as possible is a prudent strategy. The Holdridge life-zone system provides a logical basis for defining local ecosystems in a globally comparable framework. All terrestrial ecosystems can be uniquely defined in terms of three parameters: precipitation and temperature (for which data are widely accessible) and, potential evapotranspiration, which is calculated using the first two parameters (Figure 1).

Life zones can be identified roughly using existing climatic and topographic data. Overlays of satellite imagery or maps showing land-use and vegetative cover can reveal whether actual cover matches the life-zone classification. Areas that have been substantially altered by human activity can be eliminated from consideration in the foreseeable future. Lands that are largely intact do not require immediate action. This leaves at-risk areas that are partially altered or undergoing change that may respond to management interventions. Further overlay of land-capability maps will reveal where conversion to agriculture or other uses may be more appropriate. In areas where the ecosystems are at least partially intact, policy initiatives can be implemented to maintain, rehabilitate, and connect them. The identified ecosystems can then be stratified to assure that as many as possible are covered.

Forested life zones make up a majority of the blocks in Figure 1: dry forest, montane forest, humid forest, etc. All yield wood and other products of value and virtually all have been or are currently being heavily disturbed by fire and other forms of human intervention. A few sites in a variety of life zones have been managed sustainably. Intact forests represent a decreasing fraction of the potential cover. The loss or degradation of forest cover is highly uneven--among life zones, within life zones, and across countries. The drier, colder, and wetter life zones in the three corners of the diagram are least attractive for crop agriculture and therefore tend to be less disturbed. Poor countries with high population densities or with a grazing tradition tend to push disturbance further into the arid, cold, and damp corners of the diagram as well. Poverty causes the use of infertile soils and steep slopes that would be likely be left undisturbed in wealthier countries.

It is useful to note that most of the earth's surface is below 1,000 m elevation. Conversely, as one proceeds upslope in essentially conically shaped mountains, the areal extent of each succeeding life zone is smaller and more isolated from similar ecosystems on neighboring mountains. From the perspective of national planning for conservation of biodiversity this pattern is potentially important. Higher-elevation systems tend to be smaller in extent, more isolated, and potentially more threatened than some of the more extensive lowland systems and lowland rain forests may be the least threatened when compared to some upland ecosystems.

Figure 1. Diagram for the Classification of World Life Zones

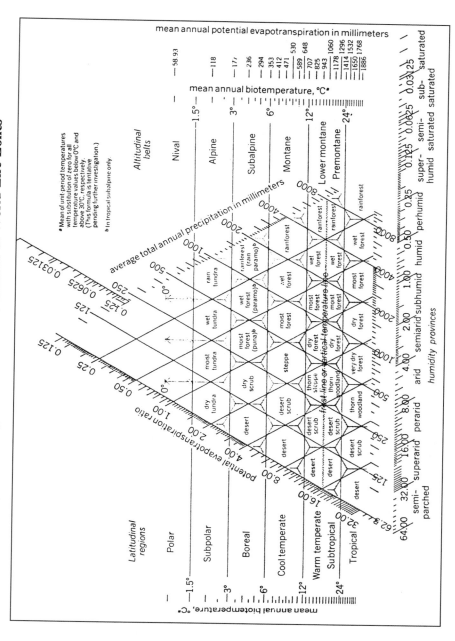

Land-Capability Assessment

A strategy for assuring that land-use is compatible with the public interest is zoning based on land-capability assessment. To the extent that restraints limit intensity of use, biodiversity maintenance is well served. A common example is the delineation of river floodplain and coastal flood-prone areas with direct prohibitions on building or control of access to flood damage insurance and services. Costa Rica, for example, legally recognizes a land-capability classification system that provides the biophysical basis for guiding credit, subsidy, and colonization programs (Tosi, 1985). That legal recognition of the classification criteria is not accompanied by widespread application is a fact of political life, but does not detract from the utility of the system once the public chooses to demand enforcement of the regulations.

The system is rooted in the widely used Holdridge classification of life zones (1967). Additional soil and slope parameters allow definition of land-use potential. Approval of credit and subsidies for agricultural and livestock production, including land clearing, can be based on objective criteria which include climatic regime, slope and soil depth, drainage, and fertility. Similarly, areas opened for colonization under land-reform programs can be limited to those where appropriate technologies can be prescribed according to existing conditions and the capacity of the land to sustain the activity in question. The more intensive use categories--intensive annual crop production, permanent crops, grazing lands, and tree crops--afford no protection to "wild" biodiversity *per se*. Significant biodiversity conservation would occur in the following categories:

(1)   *Production forest.*   Areas of high forest biomass production potential where best management practices will result in sustainable production of timber and other products. Conditions are not appropriate for other, more intensive agricultural uses.

(2)   *Extensively managed forest.* Areas with limitations not so severe as to be used solely for protection. Non-timber forest products as well as limited timber volumes can be extracted under tightly controlled conditions.

(3)   *Protection.* Areas lacking the minimal conditions for agriculture or like uses, generally steep slopes, swamps, or areas of high precipitation. These areas have high value for watershed protection, aquifer recharge, and wildlife habitat.

Financial institutions are concerned with the payment of principal and interest on credit granted. Thin, infertile soils on steep slopes with insufficient precipitation are unlikely to produce the crops and livestock needed to pay off a loan. The land-capability classification system limits government-subsidized incursions into areas that are agriculturally unproductive. This has a multiple appeal: the people and their fiscally responsible representatives have a tool to limit wasteful use of public funds on unprofitable land development schemes, the sustainable use of renewable natural resources is promoted, and the exponents of biodiversity maintenance find that these same lands remain under natural vegetative cover.

This land-capability classification system was not designed to conserve biodiversity, but rather to foster sustainable land use. In most developing countries virtually all accessible areas classified for forestry or protection would be converted to cropland and pasture, often with the encouragement of subsidies and land-settlement policies. By encouraging adherence to the last three forestry-related categories, government would foster the conservation of biodiversity over large areas currently threatened with conversion.

The system does not address the need to conserve modest representatives of ecosystems with few constraints on intensive agricultural development. It is not likely that major reserves will be created on such favored sites. Policies with associated incentives and penalties can be implemented to maintain hedgerows and stream corridors. Private conservation and tax incentives for conservation easements are discussed elsewhere in this paper. Persuading people to set aside productive land for biodiversity conservation is fairly easy in a wealthy, motivated society; the options are extremely limited in poor, overcrowded countries.

Hunting and Fishing Reserves

Kenya's Masai Mara and Costa Rica's Monte Verde cloud forest both suffer the consequences of being overloaded with nature-oriented visitors, with resultant habitat degradation, negative effects on wildlife, and loss of quality of the ecotourism experience. In contrast, the economic success of hunting reserves in such disparate locations as Zimbabwe, south Texas, and highland Ecuador attests to the appeal of

41

this land use (Williams, 1994), and the sustainability of the operation requires effective habitat maintenance, large areas, and low numbers of tourists. The hunting of trophy animals on a well-managed reserve brings tourists who pay an order of magnitude more than the photo safarist sitting back in the tourist section of the plane. The Zimbabwe example proves that appeal to wealthy clients does not preclude significant local benefits, though in general the airlines, hotels, and operators capture the bulk of the tourist's dollars. In Texas, hunting leases for deer, peccary, and quail bring a higher return than cattle while maintaining a higher-quality, more diverse habitat for these and other species. In Ecuador, deer hunting in the páramo above 3,600 meters offers a remunerative alternative or complement to the existing extensive grazing of sheep and cattle and the even more extensive uncontrolled annual burning, which creates a monotonous landscape dominated by unpalatable wire grass. Fire exclusion and management to create more browse for deer would simultaneously favor the re-establishment of a more diverse habitat for other animals as well.

Fly fishing has enjoyed (or suffered, in the eyes of the solitude-seeking angler) a boom in popularity, intensified by Maclean's *A River Runs Through It*, Redford's subsequent movie of the same name, and the more psychotherapeutic *Fly Fishing Through the Midlife Crisis*. What duck hunters through Ducks Unlimited have done for wetland habitat preservation, fly fishermen through Trout Unlimited and similar groups have accomplished for stream habitat maintenance and rehabilitation. Trout and salmon habitat maintenance is the primary tourism-oriented concern from Tierra del Fuego to Alaska, from New Zealand to Siberia, and in all cool flowing waters in between. Tiger fish in Lake Kariba, peacock bass in Amazonia, and bonefish on the mangrove-fringed flats support entrepreneurs with a vested interest in habitat maintenance. It is impressive to see a Belizean ex-commercial fisherman, now a bonefishing guide, gently but firmly insist that his client release his first bonefish.

Neither the safari outfitter nor the fishing-lodge operator has a primary interest in biodiversity conservation. The former has a two-dimensional interest in maintaining the length and breadth of the habitat for a narrow range of game animals; the primary concern of the latter is linear--the ribbon of stream or coastal habitat supporting his client's prey and its aesthetic surroundings. As for the average trout fisherman, the diverse array of benthic invertebrates anchoring the food chain supporting his beloved quarry is of but passing concern to him (Karr and Schlosser,

1978). In both cases indirect concerns are broader and activism extends to pressure on government to control land and water use affecting migrating game and fish.

If the operators have a vested interest in continued use of the resource, they will resist encroachment and be zealous pursuers of poachers, because a lost buffalo or a blasted reef represents lost profit. The long-term profitable management of any of these enterprises results in the maintenance of a good measure of the biodiversity that existed prior to human intervention. However, when profits are squeezed or intervening opportunities become more attractive, private operators will tend to intensify operations by bringing in more paying visitors, cutting corners on maintenance and protection, or simply selling out.

Private Conservation

Sherman Chickering practiced conservation of biodiversity by owning and protecting from intrusion 20,000 acres near Lake Tahoe in California (J.C. Dickinson Jr., personal communication). His action is exceptional only in the magnitude of the area set aside. Many private landowners evidence their appreciation of nature by setting aside and protecting natural areas. This has a legally defined analogue in the concept of the conservation easement, whereby the owner of land with natural vegetation cover can forgo in perpetuity the right to develop or improve the land (i.e., clear it for agriculture or urban-industrial use) in return for some form of tax relief. I have purposely used the terms "develop" and "improve" to illustrate the widely accepted convention that land with its natural cover has intrinsically a lower value to society. Reversing this public perception is a worthy task for the environmental educator.

Is the conservation-easement mechanism only applicable in economically developed countries? No, but it becomes easier to implement as a country's institutions become stronger and its population becomes more educated, more urban, and economically better off. In the somewhat more conservation-minded Brazil of today, it is doubtful that the 1970s tax rebates in the south in return for investments in rain forest clearing for cattle ranches in Amazonia would be acceptable politically. An equally ambitious rebates-for-rain-forest-conservation program could gain popular support, particularly if competitive income streams from

43

sustainable management of timber, non-timber forest products, and ecotourism could be generated.

Coral-Reef Parks, Tourists, and Fishermen

Experience in Belize (personal observation) and the Philippines indicates that creation of reef parks or fishing exclusion zones can have a positive impact on biodiversity and fish populations in and around the area set aside. In Belize, the fishing cooperative agreed to respect the creation of the 256 ha Hol Chan Reserve, encompassing 1.6 km of barrier reef and shoreward seagrass beds and mangroves off the tourist destination town of San Pedro. Within one year after the establishment of the park, a dramatic increase in the number and diversity of fishes was observed and documented over time. Fishing success in the vicinity of the park was reported to have increased. Tourist dive boats were invariably concentrated along the reef within the park boundaries where intact reefs and the most fish could be seen. Income from increased catches and from guiding tourists to the reef benefited local people.

It appears that the intact reef in the exclusion area or park serves as a refuge and a breeding and growout habitat for reef fishes. Empirical evidence has convinced fishermen that the increase in fish catch in peripheral areas warrants respecting the park boundaries. For this system to function, the fishing practices in peripheral areas must respect the physical and biological health of the whole reef and other linked ecosystems. There can be no dynamiting, poisoning, or overexploitation of the resource. Of critical importance are tenure arrangements that assure limited access to the in-shore marine resource base. The economic viability of a reef park is greatly enhanced when ecotourism can draw divers and snorkelers under carefully controlled conditions.

In populated islands, coastal areas with fringing and barrier reefs, and associated ecosystems, it will be a challenge to the ecologist, fisheries biologist, and resource economist to calculate the optimum proportion of protected to sustainably managed habitat. "Optimum" depends on which stakeholder is consulted. In Belize there are at least three interested parties:

(1) *Conservation groups.* The international and Belizean conservation groups interested primarily in establishing an extensive network of protected areas encompassing much of the coastline.

(2) *Developers*. The tourist-hotel owners, dive shops, and guides (some of whom are or were fishermen) to whom the Hol Chan Reserve represents a valuable attraction for their customers. Ironically, one developer who has devastated the mangroves near the park advertises the Reserve in the brochure for his coastal properties.

(3) *Fishermen*. The fishermen themselves who for generations have exploited the area in and around the present Reserve--trapping spiny lobster, collecting conchs, and catching fish in accordance with a complex system of inherited fishing rights.

Neither the conservation community nor the Government of Belize, even with the sympathetic support of the tourist industry, has the power to set aside and protect an extensive park system unless the fishermen are in agreement. It would appear that a practical solution is a system of protected areas that results in the maximum sustainable catch for the fisherman. The pattern of distribution and total area would be the focus of an applied research exercise involving participation by all stakeholders. There must be a pattern of alternating fishing areas with protected sites for breeding and refuge of the majority of the target species. This would not obviate the need to deal with special cases such as the concentrated breeding of grouper at a single site within a seemingly uniform habitat.

If fishermen are convinced their interests are being served, they can become a critical force in assuring that the ecological and spatial integrity of the protected areas is maintained and that the management of intervening areas is compatible with the overall production and protection goals. This assumes that the beneficiaries have exclusive access to the resource area being managed.

Alternatives to Timber Management for Biodiversity Conservation

Among the various uses of standing forests that have been proposed as being compatible with conservation are ecotourism (with or without an indigenous cultural component), extraction of non-timber forest products (fruits, medicinal materials, ornamentals, etc.), and forest management for timber.

(1) *Ecotourism*. On flights carrying Costa Ricans from San José to Disney World and returning laden with North American ecotourists,

the appeal of the exotic drives both streams--with the economic balance probably favoring Costa Rica. Ecotourism has great promise as a generator of foreign exchange while providing an economic incentive for conserving natural areas. The coming of ecotourists from abroad provides a high-profile demonstration to national decision-makers and the public that nature is valuable. The areas dedicated to ecotourism are attractive because the ecosystems are reasonably intact, the animals are relatively abundant, and the guides are effective at interpreting the landscape.

Generally a combination of primary and disturbed habitat affords the tourist the opportunity to observe the greatest diversity of landscapes, plants, and animals. The greatest advantage and disadvantage of ecotourism are that it demands so little space. As long as guides keep groups a bend in the trail or river apart, large numbers can be accommodated and still assured a quality experience. Habituated animals afford thrill after thrill to passing tourists. A visit to a local community, a small zoo, videos, and lectures make the tourism experience complete. Because ecotourism can be profitable within a few hundred or thousand hectares, there is little incentive to operators to buy or lease and protect large areas. The disadvantage is that ecotourism cannot be expected alone to justify the protection of large forest areas from conversion. Perhaps Costa Rica provides the most striking example: this small country has the world's most developed forest-based ecotourism industry, even though only a small percentage of the original forest outside of parks is still standing and the rate of deforestation is relatively high (Stewart and Gibson, n.d.). Still, even though ecotourists may not utilize large areas, awareness of the existence of extensive parks is a drawing card in countries like Ecuador (Wesche, 1995).

(2) *Extraction of non-timber products.* Historically, non-timber forest products have contributed to the meager cash income of people living in or on the fringes of forest areas, while loggers profited from timber exploitation. It is the position of some that non-timber forest products can offer an economically competitive alternative to logging and forest conversion; large extractive reserves are proposed as an effective mechanism for maintaining forest biodiversity, but this approach appears to be based more on ideology than on economics. What is provided by the extraction of non-timber forest products alone is sustained rural poverty (Browder, 1992); by any measure of well-being--income, housing, access to health care and education--the *xate* (ornamental palm)

46

and allspice gatherers of the Guatemalan Petén are unrelievedly poor. Forgoing 50 to 90 percent of the potential income stream that would derive from timber is a luxury few would willingly choose. Those engaged in extraction do not generate the surplus income needed either to pay for patrols to protect reserve borders or to pay concession fees that would allow government to protect the reserves from encroachment. These gleaners of non-timber products cover enormous areas of the forest every day, carrying their shotguns and accompanied by their dogs. If they are not to continue wreaking havoc on wildlife populations, the advocates of non-timber extraction will need to devise alternative sources of income and protein for these people.

There may be low-density populations of indigenous peoples with an extraction-based economy that have a genuine desire to live by their own traditional standards of well-being. Their reserves can effectively contribute to biodiversity conservation *if* they have political clout and sustained international support. Their case is totally different from that of migrants to the agricultural frontier who have socioeconomic aspirations similar to those of the rest of their dominant national culture.

Advocates of alternative management strategies should have the opportunity to compete for concessions on public forest lands. If governments establish concession fees based on the most remunerative sustainable use, presumably sustainable timber management, then all potential users have a common basis for bidding. The extractive bidders will presumably have to carry out international fund-raising in order to generate capital for concession fees and the costs of maintaining the integrity of the concession.

Ecotourism and non-timber forest product extraction are potentially remunerative and sustainable uses of forest systems that can contribute to biodiversity conservation. However, at the community level such uses need to be combined with timber management to assure that the overall forest-based enterprise is sustainable. An inescapable constraint is the need of every community to have long-term, well-funded NGO support, because most communities do not have the institutional structure, technical expertise, political clout, or funds to engage in sustainable, market-oriented forest-resource management. And there simply are not enough NGOs or funds to meet the grass-roots needs of forest communities.

(3) *Commercial forest management.* It is the basic hypothesis of this paper that sustainable management of forest for timber and other

products and services is a practical way to maintain forest-ecosystem biodiversity outside of parks (Dickinson, *et al.*, 1991). Most of the world's remaining forest ecosystems are found outside of parks and equivalent protected areas. Given that few of the existing parks receive adequate protection now because of lack of commitment and growing demographic and economic pressure, it is unrealistic to assume that the rest of the forest areas will be incorporated into any form of protected status.

Unfortunately, both mainstream and radical nature conservation groups find that anti-logging TV spots and literature, which reflect the perspective of many of their professional staff members, are effective for fund-raising. The stridency of these ads prejudices public opinion against all tree-cutting, whether sustainable or not. Actually, the conservationist opposition is to destructive logging, not sustainable timber management, which few have ever seen in practice. While preservation and management advocates wrangle over which strategy will save diversity, the poor farmer and cattleman are converting the forest to cropland and pasture.

It is also unfortunate that the sustainable management of forests for timber and other products and services is still being promoted primarily by other advocates of biodiversity conservation and not by the great majority of logging-company executives. Ironically, its most vociferous critics include both anti-timber advocates of biodiversity conservation and the timber and wood products industries themselves fearful that their supply of wood will be restricted. Both industry and conservationists must become convinced that sustainable timber management is profitable and one of the best available means of maintaining biodiversity outside of parks. Unless economically competitive uses for standing forests are found, they are likely to be converted to cornfields and pastures. The foremost enemy of biodiversity conservation is conversion to other uses.

A combination of compatible uses, with forest management for timber as the primary use both spatially and in terms of income generation, offers the highest potential for maintaining forest cover and a large measure of biodiversity in competition with conversion pressures. The potential for success will be far greater if (1) the policies are neutral, or preferably favorable, to long-term use of suitable land for forest production; (2) entrepreneurs and investors come to see sustainable forest management as good business within a favorable policy and regulatory setting (as they would demand if they were raising cattle or assembling computers); (3) subsidies, both national and international, can be effectively directed to paying the opportunity cost, particularly to poor people who would otherwise be attracted to the conversion option for short-term survival; (4) training and development programs are directed toward preparing people for productive involvement in forestry and complementary activities; and (5) information programs convince the public and decision-makers that forest ecosystems are beautiful and economically valuable for the goods and services they provide.

The existing situation is not pretty. Both the United States and Canada have proved that having a competent forest service and an articulate and well-funded conservation community is not sufficient to assure sustainable management of their western coniferous forests. The situation in the mixed hardwood forest of eastern North America is more promising, with longstanding examples of sustainable management. In general, however, most developed country foresters study forest management and conservation in school and practice logging after graduation. Most loggers in developing countries never studied forestry in the first place. In this context logging is simply the removal of timber from the forest with no attention to the effects of the action on regeneration, erosion, service functions, or biodiversity.

Sustained-yield management implies the removal of only the annual growth increment of the forest, extraction strategies that assure regeneration, and practices that promote maintenance of biodiversity both in the forest and downstream. The challenge is to persuade loggers to become dedicated experts in the sustainable management of forest ecosystems. This is likely to be accomplished when they become convinced that management is economically attractive and a legal condition of resource access. A critical first step is for the forest management operator to have confidence in long-term access to the resource, through either renewable concessions or secure ownership. Community industries must have confidence based on the same criteria. Becoming convinced that low-impact logging techniques are less costly than conventional practices is a relatively easy step toward voluntary sustainable management. Joint implementation agreements can actually result in the timber company's receiving a subsidy for low-impact logging (Putz, 1994). Preferential access to "green" markets is an added inducement, achievable only by conforming to all-encompassing certification criteria (Forest Stewardship Council, 1994). As major wholesalers, and even political units, begin to require certification of sustainable management, the inducement becomes more coercive. Government verification of compliance with concession requirements can provide additional pressure for sustainable management of forest resources.

By comparison with the example of the western United States and Canada, the situation in the humid and wet tropical forests of the world is actually hopeful. These forests have fewer marketable species and infrequent occurrence of even-aged stands, two conditions that make devastating clearcuts attractive, the only major exception being the dipterocarp forests of Asia, which do have a high percentage of marketable species. Paradoxically, one of the long-greatest term threats to biodiversity in tropical forests, especially in the American tropics, is underutilization. The extraction of only a tree or two per hectare leaves the forest virtually intact. This selective extraction has two distinct negative effects. First, the forest is devalued by high-grading, becoming less attractive to potential investors in sustainable timber management and, by default, more attractive to directed and spontaneous settlement. Second, most of the valuable species, like the mahoganies of America and Africa and the Asian dipterocarps, require larger gaps to reproduce than are produced in selective logging. Biodiversity is threatened if the economic competitiveness of the standing forest is reduced, making conversion a more attractive option.

Conclusion

Can biodiversity be preserved outside of officially designated parks and reserves? In developed countries the answer is a qualified yes. Well organized and funded nature conservation, fishing, and hunting organizations support biodiversity conservation, at least indirectly. These countries can afford to pay the opportunity costs required to control urban sprawl, remove grazing subsidies, consume less, and recycle more. They can afford incentives for conservation easements. These actions result in the conservation of more biodiversity. However, the general public and many politicians have only a modest interest in doing so.

In developing countries of the tropics, tiny Ecuador for example, the diversity of species is greater than in all of North America, yet the range of options for conserving this diversity is narrower. In most developing countries, the conservation movement is nascent and for the most part recently adopted and funded from abroad; biodiversity conservation is at best a slogan to a few politicians and an unknown concept among the general public. Building awareness and support is a critically important task in the long run. In the interim, pragmatic solutions must be sought. These usually do not involve overt championing of biodiversity conservation, but rather focus on making the case that the value of natural ecosystems to provide economically valuable goods and services--timber, non-timber products, clean water, etc.--is greater than if the land were converted to alternative uses. Efforts to remove incentives and revoke policies that encourage ecosystem destruction can result in biodiversity conservation without competing with immediate development needs.

References

Baskin, Yvonne. 1994. "There's a New Wildlife Policy in Kenya: Use It or Lose It." *Science*, vol. 265, Aug. 5. pp. 733-734.

BSP. 1993. *African Biodiversity: Foundation for the Future.* Washington, D.C. Biodiversity Support Program. U.S. Agency for International Development.

Browder, John. 1992. "The Limits of Extraction." *BioScience*, vol. 42, no. 3. pp. 174-182.

Dickinson, Joshua C., *et. al.* 1991. "Promising Approaches to Natural Forest Management in the American Tropics." Project report, Development Strategies for Fragile Lands. Washington, D.C. U.S. Agency for International Development.

Forest Stewardship Council. 1994. *Principles of Forest Management and Guidelines for Certifiers.* Oaxaca, Mexico. (mimeo.)

Holdridge, Leslie R. 1967. *Life Zone Ecology.* San Jose, Costa Rica. Tropical Science Center.

IUCN/UNEP/WWF. 1980. *World Conservation Strategy: Living Resources for Sustainable Development.* Gland, Switzerland. International Union for the Conservation of Nature and Natural Resources.

Karr, James R., and Isaac J. Schlosser. 1978. "Water Resources and the Land-Water Interface." *Science*, vol. 201, July 21.

Leopold, Aldo. 1949. *A Sand County Almanac: And Sketches Here and There*. New York. Oxford University Press.

Odum, Eugene P. 1975. *Ecology: The Link Between the Natural and Social Sciences*. New York. Holt, Rinehart, and Winston. pp. 53-56.

Putz, Francis E., and Michelle A. Pinard. 1993. "Reduced Impact Logging as a Carbon Offset Method." *Conservation Biology*, vol. 7, no. 4. pp. 735-737.

Shafer, Craig L. 1995. "Values and Shortcomings of Small Reserves." *BioScience*, vol. 45, no. 2. pp. 80-88.

Stewart, Rigoberto, and David C. Gibson. n.d. "The Impact of Agriculture and Forest Sector Policies on the Environment in Latin America." Washington, D.C. United States Agency for International Development. (LAC Technical Report)

Thoreau, Henry D. 1906. *Walden*. Boston, Mass. Houghton, Mifflin.

Tosi, Joseph A. 1985. *Manual para la Determinación de Capacidad de Uso de las Tierras de Costa Rica*. San José, Costa Rica. Tropical Science Center.

Wesche, Rolf J. 1995. *The Ecotourist's Guide to the Ecuadorian Amazon: Napo Province*. Quito. CEPEIGE.

Williams, Stuart. 1994. "Top of the World Whitetails." *Sporting Classics*, Nov./Dec.

Wilson, E. O. 1984. *Biophilia*. Cambridge, Mass. Harvard University Press.

Wilson, E. O. (ed). 1986. *Biodiversity*. Washington, D.C. National Academy Press.

Chapter 5

INTEGRATING PARK AND REGIONAL PLANNING THROUGH AN ECOSYSTEM APPROACH

D. Scott Slocombe*

Introduction

Protected areas have been a feature of the landscape and of the resource and environmental manager's arsenal for over a century. Today systems of protected areas seek to preserve representative samples of ecological, geological, and scenic wonders in most countries of the world. And there is growing urgency to "complete" protected-areas systems before human pressures, land-use change, and political decisions eliminate all opportunity to preserve at least samples of all of the Earth's species, habitats, and ecosystems. Protected areas, especially biosphere reserves, national and provincial parks, and World Heritage Sites, are established in part to preserve natural, unaltered ecosystems and species as benchmarks and as areas for scientific study. In addition, parks are established for public use and experience of their intrinsic values, as well as means to demonstrate the potential for coexistence of nature and human activities.

These goals often conflict; park planners and managers face difficulties reconciling conflicting goals within parks and between the parks and their surrounding regions. Traditionally, park staff have turned to ecological sciences for guidance in making policy decisions. And, indeed, ecological understanding of protected areas tells us many important things about them. It can underscore that they are dynamic and

*Acknowledgement is gratefully given for support from Wilfrid Laurier University and the Canadian Social Sciences and Humanities Research Council. Maria Kothbauer and Suzanne den Ouden were research assistants on this project.

complex systems of many interconnected and interacting components (Dolan *et al.*, 1978). The removal of one component, from a species to an entire ecosystem, can have unexpected, hard-to-predict consequences, including the numbers and distribution of species or ecosystems, or changes in physical processes and flows. Ecological understanding forces one to incorporate spatial and temporal dimensions into resource surveys, research, planning, and management (di Castri and Hadley, 1988). The pattern of activities and ecosystems in space and time is of central importance to understanding and managing a protected area. Further, ecological understanding supports assessment of the impacts of different circumstances on a protected area (Beanlands and Duinker, 1988): visitor activities, the refuse of old resource extraction activities, the effects of poaching, or the transport of pollutants in air and water from outside the boundaries. Ecological understanding highlights the fact that a protected area is subject to change and threats from both internal and external processes and activities, and that as a result management must be proactive.

Such issues are not new. But the more one applies "lessons learned" to planning and management, the more one is pushed toward a focus on entire, functioning systems rather than arbitrarily limited protected areas. Technically, this is the domain of several rapidly developing areas of research that might collectively be referred to as ecosystem science.

Ecosystem Science

The holistic, interdisciplinary study of ecosystems has been around for twenty or thirty years. It gained early impetus from the International Biological and Man and the Biosphere programs and from the work of ecologists such as E.P. and H.T. Odum (Brown *et al.*, 1980; Odum, 1983). Today there are many different but complementary approaches. Of particular relevance to parks are conservation biology, landscape ecology, ecosystem science, state-of-environment reporting, and ecological integrity (Slocombe, 1991b).

The lessons of conservation biology elaborate the implications of protected areas as islands in a sea of different land uses and strongly altered ecosystems. Such islands may have difficulty maintaining species diversity, may not incorporate functional ecosystems, and, as a result, may require intensive management of populations because of small breeding populations. Conservation biology contributes to an understanding of the dynamics of small-scale population management within isolated ecosystems (Newmark, 1987; Soulé, 1986). It provides a view of the protected area as islands from the inside looking out.

Landscape ecology provides a view of the protected area as an island from the outside looking in. It deals with the protected area as the remnant of a once much larger landscape element, now isolated in an otherwise modified landscape. It identifies the dominant landscape elements, or matrix, and identifies other islands and corridor and network features that may link islands into functionally larger systems. Landscape ecology suggests quantitative measures of landscape structure and function, and provides a framework for outlining the processes of connection and change between protected areas and other landscape elements (Forman and Godron, 1986; Gardner *et al.*, 1987; Turner, 1989).

Ecosystem science is critical to an understanding of the actual processes within particular ecosystems at various scales. Such an understanding is what permits us to anticipate and mitigate alterations caused by internal or external threats. The idea of stress/response functions in ecosystems is a particularly useful one for park managers, whose lands are almost always stressed in some way and who can often improve their recovery responses through particular interventions (Jordan *et al.*, 1987; Kothbauer, 1992; Rapport *et al.*, 1985).

A stress/response approach to park system management leads to a concern for the state of the environment in the protected area. What are the structural and functional features and characteristics of the protected area, and what is their current state? Such an assessment is critical for determining the effects of particular activities on the areas of the protected ecosystem that require more active intervention and protection. Such an approach emphasizes the need for monitoring the protected area to track change as an aid to timely intervention (GEMS, 1989). Many of these approaches can be used to collect and organize information for assessments of protected-area problems and to identify interventions needed for more effective management.

A related topic receiving much attention is "ecological integrity." It can be argued that the goal of ecosystem management should be to maintain their integrity. Indeed, since 1988 the Canadian National Parks Act makes the maintenance of ecological integrity of national parks the first priority of management. Yet ecological integrity is a difficult thing to define (e.g., Anderson, 1991). The significant quantitative work done on freshwater ecosystems (Karr, 1991) recognizes that ecosystems are complex and interconnected and have their own inherent functional and organizational properties. They draw on a range of systems and other theories to emphasize the self-organizing, self-maintaining abilities of intact ecosystems (Kay, 1991; Slocombe, 1990).

When we turn to the management of actual protected areas and their surrounding areas we are faced with other problems: "large" ecosystems, a significant human presence and activities, and the need to integrate science with planning and management activities. This is where it may be useful to speak more generally of "ecosystem approaches."

Ecosystem Approaches

Protected-area management is never simply using science to understand the protected area. Science and the understanding it brings are of necessity, parts of planning and management. But planning and management also involve institutions, administrative hierarchies, organizations, and individuals with varied goals and perceptions, all of whose interests should be reflected in the planning and management processes. Yet these processes often reflect historical, political, and disciplinary priorities and prejudices and are less inclusive and interdisciplinary than they should be. Such a priori narrowness creates problems for both scientific understanding and program implementation (e.g., Chase, 1987).

Over the last twenty years or so, in parallel with the growth of ecosystem science as described above, a number of disciplines have developed "ecosystem approaches" based on ecological and systems principles that better integrate description, understanding, and prescription in complex scientific and professional situations.

These ecosystem approaches use a holistic, interdisciplinary systems perspective and seek to place the system of primary interest in a larger context. The ecosystem is defined bioregionally or in terms of watersheds, and includes people and their activities. Ecosystem approaches focus on interactions and system behavior, and take an ecological approach to changing patterns of structure and organization. From traditions in human ecology and anthropology there is often an emphasis on linking biophysical and socioeconomic dimensions. When extended to planning and management, an ecosystem approach uses actor and institutional analyses to recommend or facilitate more consensual, participatory processes; cognitive or perceptual shifts; and institutional integration (Table 1).

Table 1. Core Characteristics of Ecosystem Approaches.

• Describing parts, systems, environments, and their interactions.
• Holistic, comprehensive, transdisciplinary.
• Including people and their activities in the ecosystem.
• Describing system dynamics, e.g., through concepts of stability, feedback, etc.
• Defining the ecosystem naturally, e.g., bioregionally, rather than arbitrarily.
• Looking at different level/scales of system structure, process, and function.
• Recognizing goals and taking an active management orientation.
• Incorporating actor-system dynamics and institutional factors in the analysis.
• Using an anticipatory, flexible research and planning process.
• Entailing an implicit or explicit ethic of quality, well-being, and integrity.
• Recognizing systemic limits to action--defining and seeking sustainability.

Source : Slocombe 1992b.

Slocombe (1991a, 1992a) presents a review of theory and experience of ecosystem approaches in a range of disciplines. At their worst such approaches blend 1960s popular "ecology" with a particular perspective on a problem. Ecosystem approaches are commonly criticized as being equilibrium-oriented, emphasizing energy flow and functionalist approaches, and neglecting historical, evolutionary, and individual factors (Moran, 1984). Yet with broad theoretical and empirical grounding, an ecosystem approach can provide a framework for organizing and integrating research, planning, and management for protected and other areas (Francis, 1988). Although interest in ecosystem management for protected areas (Agee and Johnson, 1988) has been growing, the broader ecosystem approaches as described here are less common (but see Darrow *et al.*, 1990). But interest in transdisciplinary, integrative ecosystem approaches is growing. The Canadian Government recently announced a new fifty-million-dollar program for research on large ecosystems in which human activities are central. The next section briefly presents three case studies of national-park-centered regions where various initiatives suggest possible directions for ecosystem approaches.

Case Studies

Each of the three regions discussed below includes one or more large national parks, and a mix of traditional and modern land uses. Each region needs the parks as a catalyst and as a base of economic activity. These short descriptions highlight planning and management processes that appear to be indicative of the integrative, multidisciplinary, multi-actor methods that would best facilitate an ecosystem approach to management of the region. The three regions exhibit progressively more formalized, comprehensive processes.

Kluane National Park Reserve, Yukon

Kluane National Park covers 22,015 km². Formally established in 1976, it has been a game sanctuary since 1943. Together with the adjoining Wrangell/St.Elias National Park and Preserve, it is a World Heritage Site (Slocombe, 1992a). The core of the park is the St. Elias Icefield and surrounding mountains ranging from 2,000 m to the 5,951 m Mt. Logan. The lower, outer slopes of the park are forested and include some significant lakes and marshes. They are home to some of the largest concentrations of big game found anywhere in North America.

The region has a long history of native settlement and resource harvesting. European exploration and settlement in the region were originally catalyzed at the turn of the 20th century by gold and copper mining and big-game hunting. The construction of the Alaska (Alcan) highway and the establishment of the game sanctuary ended all these activities within the protected area and created hard feelings that still exist among local inhabitants.

There is a regional population of about 1,000, 40 percent native, with a median income somewhat lower than for the Yukon as a whole. This produces strong feelings and desires for greater economic opportunities. The national park is the region's main resource, yet there are no access roads into the park and, of course, park policy precludes major hunting, trapping, and mining activity. Access was a major issue in the consultative process on updating the park management in the late 1980s. The new plan is a compromise, allowing moderate development in some less sensitive, already developed areas and formally closing the most sensitive areas to development.

In late 1987 the preparation of a Greater Kluane Regional Land-Use Plan began under joint federal, territorial, and native auspices. A Regional Planning Commission with local and government representatives was established in August 1988, and public hearings were held over the next six months to identify issues and goals. The process explicitly sought balanced development, emphasizing tourism and the highway corridor, and coordination between federal, territorial, and native planning initiatives. Although its results are only advisory, and indeed the entire program was scrapped in July 1991, the process was a unique opportunity for diverse interest groups to hear each other and consider opportunities to integrate their needs and goals.

Development of the Yukon Conservation Strategy is also significant in this regard. Led by a public working group established by the Yukon Department of Renewable Resources, it too used a public consultation process. The result was a statement intended to guide environment and development policies in the Yukon. The final strategy, released in 1990, seeks the development and sustainable use of renewable resources; a stable, healthy nonrenewable-resource sector; conservation of natural and human heritage, environmental protection; benefits and opportunities for Yukoners from resource development; community involvement in resource and conservation decision-making; and understanding aboriginal resource-management practices and knowledge.

More formally, a final umbrella agreement was reached in March 1991 on settlement of the Council of Yukon Indians' comprehensive land claim. In addition to new territory-wide planning and assessment boards and commissions, there is a specific Kluane sub-agreement. It is expected to allow Kluane native peoples to carry out subsistence harvesting in the park and game sanctuary under guidelines, to provide for 50 percent native representation on a Kluane National Park Management Board, and to grant Tribe members greater employment and training opportunities and a right of refusal on some economic development schemes.

Northern Yukon National Park

Northern Yukon National Park, in the northwest corner of the Yukon on the Beaufort Sea, covers 10,170 km^2 of gently rising arctic tundra and taiga, dissected by three major rivers flowing to the sea. The park was established in 1984 as part of the settlement of the comprehensive land claim of the western arctic Inuit Tribe. Although the nearest communities are 200 km south and southeast of the park, the area is used seasonally for subsistence harvesting by Inuvialuit and Loucheux peoples. The park is significant geomorphologically, biologically, archaeologically, and historically. It is part of the migration route of the Porcupine Caribou herd (see Parks Service, 1988; den Ouden, 1992, for details).

As part of the Inuvialuit settlement, park management goals and policies must mesh with the activities of a wide range of co-management institutions that have equal government and native representation. These include community-based hunter and trapper committees, the Inuvialuit Game Council, the Fisheries Joint Management Committee, the Wildlife Management Advisory Committee (North Slope), and the Environmental Impact Review and Impact Screening committees. Specific Inuvialuit rights with respect to the park include prior consent to changes in character or removal of park lands; advising on park planning and management; the exclusive right to harvest and dispose of game in the park; predominant employment preference and preferred rights to economic opportunities arising from park operation and management; and first refusal for wildlife guiding opportunities.

Park staff are seeking the goal of ecosystem-wide management to improve cooperation, information-sharing, and regional management by avoiding some of the existing political complications. In June 1991 the process of developing the park's first management plan was begun. A newsletter, a video, and public meetings have facilitated public input.

Regional integration and ecosystem planning concerns are significant, including the Yukon Territorial Historical Park to the north on Herschel Island, and the potential for another national park to the south as part of the Council of Yukon Indians settlement.

Also under way in 1990 and 1991 was the development of the North Yukon Regional Plan. Similar in scope to that for the Kluane region, it formally deals with lands outside the existing protected areas and emphasizes issues related to fish, wildlife, and forest management, heritage, mineral development, subsistence, and tourism. There was some desire to integrate other similar plans developed by the Inuvialuit co-management boards and the Northwest Territories Mackenzie Delta-Beaufort Sea Regional Land-Use Plan. However, this program, too, was cut in July 1991.

A biosphere reserve has been suggested as potentially useful for integrating management in the park region (Sadler, 1989). Given existing institutions and their orientations, it might be simpler to explicitly foster an ecosystem-wide orientation for existing institutions and processes.

Australian Alps National Parks

The Australian Alps National Parks comprise a contiguous 15,300 km^2 that extend from the Brindabella Ranges of Australian Capital Territory and New South Wales through the Snowy Mountains of New South Wales to the mountains of northeast Victoria and contain Australia's highest mountain, all of its mainland snowy country, a well-developed flora and fauna with many endemic species, and significant historical and archaeological sites. These so called "Australian Alps," are of national and international significance (Good, 1989).

More extensive study of the Alps program is planned, but initial research suggests it is unique. There is an explicit attempt to manage an entire ecosystem, a set of watersheds, through a system of protected areas in the region. Each of the seven national parks is managed by the appropriate state or territory government, with the federal government having some overall responsibilities such as migratory species. Although most were established in the 1970s and 1980s, one, Kosciusko National Park, was established in 1944. A review of experience there (Worboys *et al.*, 1991) identifies a number of stages over the years: a formative period that dealt with stabilization and constituency-building without addressing major conflicts; then a period of conflict resolution through active management in the 1960s; a period of professionalization of the parks service in the 1970s, followed by community involvement and political pressures in the 1980s. The 1990s are expected to bring commercialization and increasing cooperative efforts with governments, communities, and private interests.

Cooperative management emerged in the early 1980s in response to observed needs and opportunities to create a conservation framework for a nearly contiguous area in the Alps. The first Memorandum of Understanding (MOU) between the relevant governments was signed in 1986. Its implementation is guided by the Alps Liaison Committee, a group of senior administrators from the governments involved, which prepares an annual works program and a report and is responsible for achieving the objectives of the MOU. As the administration and management of the MOU have evolved, improvements have been made: a three-year work program with commitment of funds by governments, secondment of a full-time officer to manage the cooperative program, the establishment of specialist working groups, and the identification of lead agencies for particular projects (Worboys *et al.*, 1991).

The benefits of the program have included an Alps map and poster; bushwalking and horse-riding codes; a major symposium and reports on the scientific significance, heritage, and cultural heritage of the Alps; a bibliography on the Alps; and cooperative training and fire management programs. All these are excellent, concrete contributions to ecosystem management, not yet evident in the other regions examined. Potential improvements are seen in making cooperative ventures routine, devolving management to the operational level, increasing uniformity of standards across the whole Alps, and ensuring long-term commitments to the resolution of difficult issues, perhaps through legislating the MOU.

As the land managers focus on protecting biodiversity, achieving regional integration, and on maintaining ecosystem integrity and traditional uses, ecosystem-wide management will become more and more common. This will increasingly require new scientific and administrative methods and processes, ecosystem approaches, and complex administrative regimes such as the above examples illustrate.

Conclusions

Conceiving of protected areas as complex, changing, connected systems at several scales is an important first step towards effective ecosystem-wide management. The second step is developing research and monitoring methods to increase our understanding of protected areas as

Table 2. Advantages of an ecosystem approach to protected-area planning/management

- integrates socioeconomic and biophysical dimensions into research and management

- integrates research and planning and management

- considers whole, functional ecosystems and their characteristics

- facilitates goal-oriented process

- encourages participation and learning from all actors

- facilitates integration of scientific, actor, and institutional dimensions in to the design

islands, as distinct systems responding to stresses, whose overall ecosystem integrity needs to be maintained. Empirical and scientific research can form the basis of an "ecosystem approach" to planning and management that should guide research and monitoring and facilitate their integration into effective, implemented, sustainable interventions.

Such an ecosystem approach can contribute a number of specific advantages to protected-area planning and management (Table 2). The importance of this approach is underscored by experience with biosphere reserves. Successful ones are successful not because of their designation, but because of the development of a multidisciplinary, multi-actor process for guiding and integrating research and management in a whole regional ecosystem.

At the same time as protected areas are coming to be seen as critical elements in efforts to protect the biosphere, they are increasingly under threat of change from internal and external causes. Ecosystem science and ecosystem approaches can contribute much to improved planning and management in this context (Slocombe, 1992b). In the long

63

term, protected areas must do more than protect, biodiversity, and natural wonders. They must also help to integrate conservation and development and thus contribute to sustaining societies (McNeely and Miller, 1984).

References

Agee, J.K., and D.R. Johnson (eds.). 1988. *Ecosystem Management for Parks and Wilderness*. Seattle. University of Washington Press.

Anderson, Jay E. 1991. "A Conceptual Framework for Evaluating and Quantifying Naturalness." *Conservation Biology*, vol. 5, no. 3. pp. 347-352.

Beanlands, G.E., and P.N. Cuinker. 1983. *An Ecological Framework for Environmental Impact Assessment in Canada*. Ottawa. Federal Environmental Assessment and Review Office.

Brown, J., *et al.* 1980. *An Arctic Ecosystem: The Coastal Tundra at Barrow, Alaska*. Stroudsburg, Pa. Dowden, Hutchinson, and Ross.

Chase, Alston. 1987. *Playing God in Yellowstone: The Destruction of America's First National Park*. New York. Harcourt, Brace, Jovanovich.

Darrow, G.F., *et al.* 1990. "Crown of the Continent Project." Montana. Glacier National Park. (ms.)

den Ouden, S. 1992. *CoManagement and Ecosystem Planning in the Mackenzie Delta Yukon North Slope Region*. Waterloo, Ont. Wilfrid Laurier University. (B.A. thesis in Geography)

di Castri, F., and M. Hadley. 1988. "Enhancing the Credibility of Ecology: Interacting Along and Across Hierarchical Scales." *GeoJournal*, vol. 17, no. 1. pp. 535.

Dolan, R., B.P. Hayden, and G. Soucie. 1978. "Environmental Dynamics and Resource Management in the U.S. National Parks." *Environmental Management*, vol. 2, no. 3. pp. 249-258.

Forman, R.T.T., and M. Godron. 1986. *Landscape Ecology*. New York. Wiley.

Francis, G.R. 1988. "Institutions and Ecosystem Redevelopment in Great Lakes America with Reference to Baltic Europe." *Ambio*, vol. 17, no. 2. pp. 106-111.

Gardner, R.H., *et al.* 1987. "Neutral Models for the Analysis of Broadscale Landscape Pattern." *Landscape Ecology*, vol. 1, no. 1. pp. 19-28.

GEMS Monitoring and Assessment Research Centre. 1989. *Environmental Data Report,* 2nd ed. Oxford, U.K. Basil Blackwell.

Good, Roger (ed.). 1989. *The Scientific Significance of the Australian Alps.* Canberra. Australian Alps National Parks Liaison Committee and Australian Academy of Science.

Jordan, W.R., III, M.E. Gilpin, and J.D. Aber (eds.). 1987. *Restoration Ecology.* Cambridge, U.K. Cambridge University Press.

Karr, J.R. 1991. "Biological Integrity: A Long Neglected Aspect of Water Resource Management." *Ecological Applications*, vol. 1, no. 1. pp. 66-84.

Kay, J.J. 1991. "A Nonequilibrium Thermodynamic Framework for Discussing Ecological Integrity." *Environmental Management*, vol. 15, no. 4. pp. 483-495.

Kothbauer, Maria. 1992. *National and Provincial Park Management Responses to External Threats in Ontario.* Waterloo, Ont. Wilfrid Laurier University. (M.A. thesis in Geography)

McNeely, J.A., and K.R. Miller (eds.). 1984. *National Parks, Conservation and Development.* Washington, D.C. Smithsonian Institution Press.

Moran, E.F. 1984. *The Ecosystem Concept in Anthropology.* Washington, D.C. American Association for the Advancement of Science.

Newmark, W.D. 1987. "A Land-Bridge Island Perspective on Mammalian Extinctions in Western North American Parks." *Nature*, vol. 325, no. 6103, 29 January. pp. 430-432.

Odum, H.T. 1983. *Systems Ecology: An Introduction.* New York. Wiley.

Parks Service [Canada]. 1988. *Northern Yukon National Park: Interim Management Guidelines.* Winnipeg. Prairie and Northern Region.

Rapport, D.J., H.A. Regier, and T.C. Hutchinson. 1985. "Ecosystem Behavior Under Stress." *American Naturalist*, vol. 125, no. 5. pp. 617-640.

Sadler, Barry. 1989. "National Parks, Wilderness Preservation, and Native Peoples in Northern Canada." *Natural Resources Journal*, vol. 29, no. 1. pp. 185-204.

Slocombe, D.S. 1990. "Assessing Transformation and Sustainability in the Great Lakes Basin." *GeoJournal*, vol. 21, pp. 251-272.

Slocombe, D.S. 1991. *An Annotated, Multidisciplinary Bibliography of Ecosystem Approaches.* Waterloo, Ont., and Sacramento, Cal. Wilfrid Laurier University Cold Regions Research Centre and IUCN/CESP.

Slocombe, D.S. 1992a. "Environmental Monitoring for Protected Areas: Review and Prospect." *Environmental Monitoring and Assessment*, vol. 21, no. 1. pp.49-78.

Slocombe, D.S. 1992b. "The Kluane/Wrangell St. Elias National Parks, Yukon and Alaska: Seeking Sustainability through Biosphere Reserves." *Mountain Research and Development*, vol. 12, no. 1. pp. 63-70.

Slocombe, D.S. 1993. "Environmental Planning, Ecosystem Science, and Ecosystem Approaches for Integrating Environment and Development." *Environmental Management*, vol. 17, no. 3. pp. 289-303.

Soulé, M.E. (ed.). 1986. *Conservation Biology: The Science of Scarcity and Diversity.* Sunderland, Mass. Sinauer Associates.

Turner, M.G. 1989. "Landscape Ecology: the Effect of Pattern on Process." *Annual Review of Ecology and Systematics*, vol. 20. pp. 171-197.

Worboys, G.L., *et al.* 1991. "Protected Area Management in the Australian Alps: A Case Study: Kosciusko National Park." In L.S. Hamilton, D.P. Bauer, and H.F. Takeuchi (eds.). *Parks, Peaks, and People.* Honolulu, Hawaii. East-West Center Program of Environment.

Chapter 6

TECHNIQUES FOR RESOLVING CONFLICT IN NATURAL RESOURCE MANAGEMENT

Edwin E. Krumpe and Lynn McCoy

Introduction

Managers of parks and protected areas are faced with mounting pressures to make resource decisions that balance the competing needs of a growing population with a dwindling base of natural resources (Crowfoot and Wondolleck, 1990). It is only natural that conflicting viewpoints should arise about how to manage and utilize these resources. Successful long-term management of public lands requires a degree of trust between government agencies, private interests, and the public that can be developed through a public participation process that is truly accessible, responsive, and interactive.

The five techniques discussed in this paper were use by several public task forces created to develop management plans and solve conflicts between competing uses in United States parks and protected areas. These include areas such as the Snake River in Hells Canyon National Recreation Area in Idaho (Krumpe and McCoy, 1991), the Metolius River Conservation Area in Oregon, the Arkansas River Recreation Area in Colorado (BLM, 1988), and the Jedediah Smith Wilderness in Wyoming. The conflicts addressed included competing recreation uses, grazing, timber harvest, fish and wildlife, mineral extraction, and historic preservation. The techniques described can be used in any regional planning exercise that looks towards a logical resolution of conflicting needs and interests.

Experience in the United States has shown that a public task force or advisory group is often a very useful way to resolve conflicts and to assist managers in making planning and management decisions. The techniques for task-force decision-making outlined in this paper are designed specifically to provide members of the public with an opportunity to shape planning decisions for parks and protected areas. These techniques include setting guidelines for selecting task-force members, defining responsibilities and operating rules, using a four-level approach to consensus decision-making, using a positive method for identifying issues and mutually acceptable goals, and rotating small groups to develop management actions and solve contentious issues.

Set Guidelines for Selecting Task-Force Members

Selecting the members of the task force is an important first step. Quality decision-making depends upon the participation of a full spectrum of public interests. It is important to first identify interest groups (those who have a stake in the future of the resource) and then identify specific people who can represent those groups on the task force.

Task-force members should be selected to represent diverse groups even though they will have varied views on management objectives and the methods of achieving them. This is important because decisions that are developed and supported by a diverse task force will usually be acceptable to the public at large. The following guidelines should be followed to select task force members:

(1) Ensure that a diversity of interest groups are represented, including recreation user groups, affected government agencies, nature enthusiasts, tourism operators, local business interests, academia, and others.

(2) Include those with veto power (the power to block management decisions) and those who have the authority to represent their group.

(3) When possible, allow the interest groups to choose their own representatives; when this is not feasible, consult with a variety of groups representing a given interest.

(4) Select people who are well known within their organizations and among other groups as well.

(5) Select people who are willing to listen, negotiate, compromise, and communicate.

(6) Select a group that is well balanced and has equal or balanced representation of different interests.

68

(7) Limit the size of the task force, to permit an easy exchange of personal and technical knowledge (20 people or fewer, not including alternates).

Define Responsibilities and Procedures

The responsibilities of the task-force members need to be defined, so as to avoid wasting time and energy discussing topics outside of the responsibility of the planning effort. It is also important for task-force participants to understand what their responsibilities are before committing to participate.

At the first meeting, the task force members should review a list of responsibilities and procedures that will guide their conduct. They should be free to either adopt or modify the list. By doing so, all members will know and agree to what is expected of them. As a set of guidelines for their meetings, past task force groups have agreed to:

(1) Represent their interest groups and report back to their constituency.

(2) Attend the meetings, keep their alternates informed, and tell the facilitator if they cannot attend a meeting.

(3) Be willing to work in a team setting and be open to discussion and understanding a wide range of viewpoints.

(4) Give everyone a chance to speak and withhold judgment on an idea presented by others until it has a chance to be developed.

(5) Focus on ideas and issues, *not* on people or their personalities. Be open-minded and not take firm positions as a starting point for discussions.

(6) Strive to reach consensus at decision points.

(7) Allow their names to be made public so that other people with similar interests can relay their views.

(8) Speak *concisely* and listen without interrupting.

(9) If problems or concerns arise about how the task force is operating, make these known to the task force or facilitator first and attempt to resolve them within the task-force structure.

The ninth guideline is particularly important because when individuals air their concerns or complaints to outsiders it often serves to undermine the mutual trust and respect among members that is important to the process of reaching consensus on decisions.

Use the "Four Levels for Support" to Reach Consensus

The task force should not ordinarily vote, but should attempt to decide by consensus. The basic tool for reaching consensus should be a group learning process where participants gain an appreciation of the needs and views of others (Friedmann, 1987). The best strategy will be to identify points of agreement and build upon these. Points of disagreement should be isolated and dealt with within the task-force setting in a straightforward and positive manner.

The idea of consensus is central, because taking votes implies that a simple majority rules and thus that almost half of the members may not support the decision. This hinders progress toward developing mutually acceptable goals (Avery *et al.*, 1981). Furthermore, people tend to notice who is voting "against" them, and compromise or cooperation may then be blocked. It is far better for people to work together until they can reach a decision that all can accept, even if it is not their first choice.

At key decision-making points, it is helpful to ask task-force members to express their level of support for consensus on an issue or proposed action by indicating one of four levels of support:

   (1) I can easily support the action.
   (2) I can support the action but it may not be a preference.
   (3) I can support the action if minor changes are made.
   (4) I cannot support the action unless major changes are made.

This technique allows the group to assess quickly how close they are to reaching consensus. If the members have Level 4 concerns, discussion will continue. Level 3 concerns will have to be addressed so that they do not become Level 4 concerns at decision points. Consensus will be defined as no one's having a Level 4 concern about the action in question.

Where disagreement occurs on an issue, the member with a Level 4 concern should be asked to focus on the wording--tell the group how he or she would reword the decision to make it more acceptable. By concentrating on wording, the group must focus on reaching a solution rather than dwelling on philosophical points of disagreement.

Use a Positive Approach to Identify Issues and Set Goals

Conflict in natural-resource management often results from people's focusing on differing viewpoints regarding what is the best way to use resources associated with parks and protected areas. The key to conflict resolution is to have individuals reach a shared viewpoint. The first step in achieving this is to build upon the positive values that people bring to the task force.

All too often the typical scenario for resolving conflicts is to have everyone identify what he or she thinks are the issues. The manager then attempts to develop management actions that will address these issues. The problem with this approach is that by first identifying issues, the task force will be likely to focus on negative aspects of problems and the differences among members. This may lead to polarization and to labeling or stereotyping other members, which in turn deters the cooperation, mutual understanding, and trust upon which consensus decisions can best be made. An alternative approach is to start by pointing out to members why they are meeting together--because they all care about the resources of the park or protected area. This shared value can become the cornerstone from which to build understanding, respect, and eventually cooperation and consensus.

One approach to building mutual understanding among members is to use a technique that emphasizes their common values. Begin by requesting that task force members silently write down a list of things that they like or value about the park or protected area. Particularly, they should identify values they feel should be maintained, protected, or achieved. It may be helpful to ask them to envision their ideal for the future of the protected area.

The next step is to go around the group and ask each member, in turn, to present one value from his or her list. Continue going around the group until everyone's values have all been read out. These values are written on large paper in front of the group. Although this seems like a simple process, it is important because members discover that people from different interest groups share some of the same values they

71

do. Task-force members quickly realize that the resource is valued by many people for many reasons. Furthermore, this list is useful throughout the entire conflict resolution process to refocus people on the values they want to see maintained, protected, or achieved.

Only after the members have identified the values they hold about the park or protected area should they begin to identify issues. The identification of issues can be developed in a positive manner by asking members to list what they think could be potential threats to their values. Having listened to what each other's values are, members will be more likely to understand what other people believe to be issues or threats.

At this point the group is ready to begin developing goals and objectives which will lead to the formulation of management actions. This is accomplished by asking the group to write specific goals and objectives that address the threats identified and protect the values. For example, a goal may be to perpetuate a particular animal species that is valued by the public. Specific objectives might include reducing poaching and providing a better opportunity for visitors to view the animals. The task force can now begin to develop specific management actions to accomplish these objectives.

Use a Team Rotation Technique to Develop Management Actions

A team rotation technique can maximize opportunities for individual involvement. It is important to realize that the best decisions are reached when all the task-force members are involved in making the decisions. It quickly becomes apparent that not everyone's opinion on every topic can be expressed in a meeting of the entire task force. Some people may feel intimidated by the prospect of speaking in front of a large group while others may tend to dominate the conversation. One way to encourage individual participation, group discussion, and the expression of ideas is by using a team rotation technique.

The task-force members should be divided into small teams composed of varied interest groups. Each team will be assigned one or more of the different goals and objectives for which they must write suggested management actions. After a fixed time (20 to 30 minutes) the groups rotate stations, leaving their lists behind them. At the second station they examine the list from the initial group and then write additional proposals for management actions or suggest modifications.

They continue rotating in this fashion until they return to their original station. Here they study what the other groups have suggested and then rewrite the proposal to encompass comments from the other teams. These are brought before the full group for discussion and ratification. After participating in this rotation technique, it is much simpler for the group as a whole to discuss and ratify the suggested management actions.

The advantages of the small-team rotation technique are that all the participants are given the opportunity to express their opinion on every topic and to learn what other people's opinions are. This is in contrast to the traditional approach in which specialized subcommittees are formed to discuss one topic and develop recommendations in isolation. Rotating in mixed groups promotes fuller participation and a better sharing of information. This technique can be used at any point in the task-force process to discuss issues and develop solutions efficiently.

Conclusion

The preceding five techniques have proved helpful in resolving conflicts in the planning and management of parks and protected areas in the United States. Additional conflict resolution techniques can be found in Krumpe and McCoy (1991), Doyle and Straus (1982), Crowfoot and Wondolleck (1990), Avery et al. (1981), Auvine et al. (1978), Delbeque (1985), and Friedmann (1987).

Using a task force will ensure that better decisions are made and will increase the likelihood that these decisions will be acceptable to the public. Members should be selected who can represent and speak for a broad range of interests. The role and responsibilities of the task force should be clearly defined and agreed upon. Decisions should be made by consensus. Issues should be developed in a positive manner and opportunities should be provided for all members to participate fully. With these five techniques for conflict resolution, managers can build partners and advocates for better management of natural resources.

References

Avery, Michel, et al. 1981. *Building United Judgement: A Handbook for Consensus Decision Making.* Madison, Wisc. Center for Conflict Resolution.

Auvine, Brian, *et al.* 1978. *A Manual for Group Facilitators*. Madison, Wisc. Center for Conflict Resolution.

Crowfoot, James E., and Julia Wondolleck. 1990. *Environmental Disputes, Community Involvement in Conflict Resolution*. Washington, D.C. Island Press.

Doyle, Michael, and David Straus. 1982. *How to Make Meetings Work*. New York. Berkley.

Delbeque, Andre L., Andrew H. Van de Ven, and David H. Gustafson. 1975. *Group Techniques for Program Planning: A Guide to Nominal Group and Delphi Process*. Glenview, Ill. Scott, Foresman.

Friedmann, John. 1987. *Planning in the Public Domain: From Knowledge to Action*. Princeton, N.J. Princeton University Press.

Krumpe, Edwin E., and Lynn McCoy (eds.). 1991. *Limits of Acceptable Change: Recreation Management Plan for the Snake River in Hells Canyon National Recreation Area*. Moscow, Idaho. University of Idaho. (Idaho Forest, Wildlife and Range Experiment Station, Publication No. 624)

BLM. 1988. *Arkansas River Management Plan*. Denver. Colorado State Office, Bureau of Land Management.

74

Chapter 7

STRENGTHENING REGIONAL PLANNING THROUGH COMMUNITY EDUCATION

Nina M. Chambers and Sam H. Ham

Introduction

The conservation movement has embraced the idea that protected areas cannot exist as islands, but are a part of a larger, more complex landscape. Experts (see, for example, MacKinnon *et al.*, 1986) argue that protected areas are just one type of specialized land use within a landscape mosaic. Therefore, it is unlikely that protected areas alone will be successful in conserving biodiversity if they are surrounded by degraded habitats that limit gene flow, alter nutrient and water cycles, and lead to regional and global climate change (McNeely, 1993). As Lovejoy (1984) pointed out, the integrity of the surrounding landscape also needs to be maintained if the biological systems inside protected areas are to be preserved. Clearly, regional planning at a landscape level is critical to the long-term protection of ecosystem processes, and rural communities directly dependent on these processes must be recognized as part of the ecological landscape.

Incorporating rural communities into the regional planning process and understanding their relationship within the landscape is critical. The biosphere reserve concept is based on the idea that local people are a part of the landscape and have much to offer in terms of traditional knowledge and experience in traditional land uses (von Droste and Gregg, 1985). According to MacFarland (1984) and others (e.g., Nietschmann, 1984; IUCN *et al.*, 1979), the reserve can be a forum for additional training and education aimed at improving resource management practices and demonstrating appropriate land uses. Central to biosphere reserves is the buffer-zone concept, which incorporates local people and land-use systems into a larger conservation planning framework. Ham *et al.* (1989) argued that buffer zones and protected areas can offer strategic environmental education opportunities for a variety of audiences, thereby enhancing the link between the community and the landscape.

The Importance of Community Participation in Land-Use Planning

Community participation in local land management is important to the long-term success of conservation at a regional level. A prevailing notion is that community-based approaches to planning tend to be more effective because they incorporate the relevant knowledge and experience of those affected by land-use decisions (e.g., Brandon and Wells, 1992; McNeely, 1993). In this way, participation can help to mitigate potential and existing conflicts and empower the community to take a more active role in exploring management issues and initiating possible responses.

Community empowerment is both desirable and critical to the success of collaborative management (McNeely, 1993). According to Renard (1991a) and Jacques (1986), it serves four main purposes: (1) it promotes democracy and equality with equal opportunity to share in decisions, (2) it increases economic and technical efficiency because resource users have more clearly defined responsibilities for their actions, (3) it is adaptive and responsive to variation in local social and environmental conditions (locals are able to respond to changes more quickly than outsiders are), and (4) it increases stability and commitment to management that central government cannot duplicate.

The function of community participation can be viewed from two broad perspectives--coercive or interactive. The difference between these perspectives is the level of input from, or power given to, the community. In the coercive approach, protected-area managers try to "sell" the idea of protection to the communities because they feel the protected areas are doomed unless local communities "buy into" them. The interactive point of view is that sustainable development and benefits to the protected area and surrounding communities are possible only to the extent that local people are involved.

In the coercive perspective, community participation in land management is seen as an important enforcement (check and balance) mechanism to control natural-resource depletion (Wind, 1991). For example, Brown et al. (1992) describe the communities around a protected area as being in a "bargaining zone" where locals, managers, development agencies, and non-governmental organizations (NGOs) bargain with each other to achieve their own objectives. However, since the bargaining power of the community is generally less than that of the management agency, the education and training offered to communities is often biased toward the perceptions and goals of the management agency rather than the needs of the community.

The interactive approach, which focuses on community-identified education and training priorities, may be better in the long term because it relies on the concept of "co-management," incorporates community participation at a higher level and gives the community greater control over its own destiny. Renard and Hudson (1992) define co-management as simply "sharing of management authority and responsibilities by governments and communities." In their view, a partnership is created in which rights, aspirations, knowledge, and skills are respected and enhanced, and in which the importance of human-nature relationships is recognized and valued. In addition to traditional natural-resource questions, relevant social issues raised by the community may include traditional land-use patterns or methods, territorial rights, or the right to self-determination. Besides these social aspects of environmental management, the economic side of integrated development planning is also important, and experience has shown that it may be particularly important in tourism planning where cultures and environmental quality are central concerns (Renard, 1991b; McLaughlin *et al.*, 1992). Not all communities, however, are equipped to participate fully at the co-management level; they may need additional education to build experience and to strengthen confidence that problems can be confronted and solved locally.

(1) *Bridging an information gap.* Effective participation by communities may require improving technical knowledge within the community and improving communications between the community and other institutions with an aim toward collaboration and institutional strengthening. Through these different modes of education, communities may be empowered to participate in management as partners with established management agencies. However, it is not only the community that needs additional training and education. Government agencies, NGOs, and assistance agencies also may need training and education to foster collaboration and co-management. Clearly, how such training is planned and implemented will determine its chances for success.

(2) *Opinions on community participation and co-management.* Recent literature on community participation in natural-resources

77

management shows an evolution from a coercive to a more interactive approach, with the ultimate goal of co-management. Rocheleau (1991), Drake (1991), Wind (1991), Renard (1990), and Jacques (1986) all discuss different levels of participation, ranging from community-provided local labor at the lowest level to community management and evaluation of projects at the highest level. According to Rocheleau, a key difference among the levels is the extent to which a community has equality in the exchange of information and responsibility with the other management agencies.

In the 1980s, the literature discussing community participation centered largely around mitigating threats through compensation (e.g., von Droste and Gregg, 1985; Garrett, 1984; Machlis and Tichnell, 1985) and extracting information from locals or giving them information (Thelen and Child, 1984). In contrast, the literature of the last few years places more attention on the integral nature of rural communities within the local landscape, empowerment, community decision-making, and co-management. Barzetti (1993), for example, identifies the new trend in protected-area management as dominated by stronger community involvement and greater institutional collaboration than ever before.

Since inception of the biosphere-reserve concept, acceptance of human settlements as part of the landscape has steadily grown. The IUCN Caracas Declaration (McNeely, 1993) clearly elevates community management in protected-area management to a new level of importance. Norton and Ulanowicz (1992) discuss biodiversity conservation in terms of "human values" of the landscape, a notable departure from a strictly biological point of view. And central to this new paradigm is the importance of community participation in conservation management (see, for example, Rowntree, 1992; Wind, 1991; and Jacques, 1986).

Opportunities for co-management can be associated with education and training, and protected areas and buffer zones in particular offer strategic environmental education opportunities for several different groups, including local decision-makers and opinion leaders (Ham et al., 1989). Appropriately delivered programs aimed at key audiences may help in community-strengthening efforts. Participatory processes, and building upon what is learned through them, catalyze development by empowering local people and institutions to take positive actions in their own behalf, thus rising to the level of co-management.

Although the ideal of co-management may appear basic to land-use planning, achieving it in a real-world setting is often more complex. Real-life limitations of politics, history, economic forces, and cultural traditions determine to a large extent not only what is needed but the range of possibilities.

Planning and Implementing Educational Programs: Jamaica Case Study

In a recent case study, we examined co-management possibilities in a portion of a buffer zone between the Blue and John Crow Mountains National Park and the proposed Port Antonio Marine Park in northeast Jamaica. Our purpose was to bring together local communities and conservation organizations in an effort to combine conservation goals with community development goals, and to encourage interinstitutional collaboration to achieve these goals.

One component of the study looked at land use and land cover within the buffer zone in order to recommend a conservation corridor connecting the terrestrial and marine ecosystems. The proposed corridor includes several small villages and tourism attractions in a nearly continuous band of vegetation including remnants of natural ecosystems, second-growth forests, and mixed-crop agricultural zones. Recent lessons from conservation biology and island biogeography (see, for example, Gorman, 1979; Csuti, 1991) suggest that the designation of such a corridor may help to protect the ecosystems it contains (including the watersheds affecting the marine park) and to control development within this zone that could have a negative impact on the two parks.

A related component of the study involved a participatory planning process in a small rural community, called Nonsuch, within the buffer zone and proposed corridor (Figure 1). The purpose of the exercise was to help identify local development goals compatible with the parks. The participatory process focused on the empowerment of local leaders and the community organization to take more control of their destiny and to explore other opportunities they may not have been aware of previously. This process was facilitated by the researcher and guided by the community group--the Nonsuch Citizens Association.

The planning process began with community members identifying values they held about their local environment. These values included a clean environment, natural beauty, and availability of water. Next, they set acceptable criteria (or boundaries) on potential change that might

79

result from development in the community and affect the values they had identified. From this foundation, the group then set broad goals from which specific objectives and corresponding projects to achieve these goals were identified. The process culminated with a workshop that brought the community into contact with representatives of donor and other assistance agencies in order to encourage collaboration. The agencies represented a wide range of organizations, including local and national NGOs, government agencies, private-sector agencies (including loan agencies), and community-group representatives from several other villages on the island.

**Figure 1. Participatory planning in the community
of Nonsuch, Jamaica**

Data were gathered throughout the study from interviews, maps, and aerial photography. Two journals were kept by the researcher. One documented the results of meetings and steps taken in the community planning process; the other was used for daily entries regarding perceived reactions of community members to the planning process, and for observations of the perceptions different agency representatives had of each other and the perceptions of their agencies by the community.

Structured, open-ended interviews were held with decision-makers from sixteen institutions involved in environmental issues in the study area. These included government agencies, quasi-public agencies, United States Government representatives, local and national NGOs, and the other international organizations working in the area and involved in environmental decision-making in Jamaica (see Table 1). The interviews sought to identify the values, threats, issues, priorities for action, and long-term goals perceived by each group as important within the buffer zone.

Table 1. Institutions Interviewed as Part of the Case Study

TYPE OF INSTITUTION	SPECIFIC INSTITUTIONS
Government of Jamaica	Natural Resources Conservation Authority, Blue and John Crow Mountains National Park, Protected Areas Resource Conservation Project (administered by the Planning Institute of Jamaica)
Quasi-public	Conservation Data Centre (at the University of the West Indies), Port Antonio Chamber of Commerce, Jamaica Tourist Board
United States Government	United States Agency for International Development, United States Peace Corps
Non-governmental organizations	Jamaica Conservation and Development Trust, Portland Environmental Protection Association, National Environmental Societies Trust, proposed Port Antonio Marine Park
International Organizations	United Nations Environment Programme, Organization of American States, The Nature Conservancy, Rio Grande Valley Project (funded and co-administered by the Dutch Government)

The result of this effort was a document that defines a conservation corridor linking the two parks. In addition, the document included management recommendations for the corridor and parks. Also incorporated were a community development plan that resulted from the participatory planning process and a synthesis which pulled together both the conservation and community development goals that had been identified.

Table 2. Potential Types of Education and Delivery Systems for Various Target Audiences

TRAINING	TYPE OF EDUCATION OR TARGET GROUP	DELIVERY SYSTEMS
Community members	general environmental education; technical training in agriculture or other land-use or income-generating activities	appropriate mass media, such as radio extension, demonstration, practical experience and training workshops
Local NGOs	improved communication skills to target new audiences; institutional strengthening (record- keeping skills, fundraising, and project development) ways to network between groups to increase awareness and collaboration; extension techniques	seminars training in small groups practical experience in collaborative projects with community groups
National and international NGOs, government agencies, private-sector organizations	extension and community development skills; exploration of opportunities for collaboration and resulting mutual benefit	training interinstitutional workshops
Donor agencies	small community needs and an appropriate scale and duration of assistance; practical application	interinstitutional workshops case study experiences

From this case study emerged three broad questions related to encouraging community participation and improving community education and training. These are: (1) who needs to be educated? (2) what kinds of education are needed? and (3) how should education and training be conducted? As Wood and Wood (1990) and Ham *et al.* (1993) have argued, education and training must be targeted at key institutions and population segments that may have strategic roles in the diffusion of local knowledge and the adoption of new practices. The key audiences identified in Jamaica, the types of training needed by each, and representative delivery systems are listed in Table 2. The remainder of this discussion is organized around the above three questions and their possible implications for Jamaica and elsewhere.

Who needs to be educated? The case-study interviews revealed environmental education of rural people as one of the two most frequently cited approaches for mitigating threats within the buffer zone. In Jamaica, as elsewhere in the Caribbean, there are some constraints on community participation. As in other post-colonial plantation societies, community cohesion tends to be low (Espeut, 1990). Among the constraints identified at the Caribbean Regional Workshop on People's Participation in Development and the Management of Natural Resources (Saint Lucia, 1985) are illiteracy, unemployment, tribalism created by partisan politics, the absence of institutional mechanisms to address imbalances between minority and majority rights, the historically severe exploitation of resources, and the heightened impact of external events on local conditions. The impact of these constraints is evidenced by Espeut's (1990) observation that many production cooperatives have failed in Jamaica because of weak local leadership, lack of trust among members, and Jamaican individualism. Quite possibly, some of these constraints might be overcome through positive experiences in solving problems by communities working together. Overcoming these constraints is necessary if communities are to work successfully together in decision-making.

Local opinion leaders constitute an important audience for education programs. Opinion leaders are typically those few persons in the community whom other members of the community respect and trust. Often, however, they have a difficult time garnering and maintaining support because they lack a concrete sense of how to capitalize on possible sources of assistance external to the community. For example, the Nonsuch Citizens Association has experienced wide fluctuations in community support because it has had little success in securing outside assistance for needed projects. Local leaders need to be strengthened to become aware of the wide range of co-management possibilities that exist. There needs to be a greater awareness of the responsibilities they have, or could have, in controlling the development of their own communities. In Nonsuch, people who rise to community leadership positions are sometimes perceived as doing so primarily for personal benefit. This perception is discouraging to new potential leaders and diminishes the support and involvement of the rest of the community. Community leaders need to be encouraged and new leaders brought along to their level. Improving how communities perceive leadership will also facilitate greater participation and help to create a more cohesive group that will be better positioned to achieve its development goals.

Institutions that may be able to assist rural communities in conservation and development are another important audience for education programs. These may include government agencies, NGOs, private businesses, and donor organizations, which in many cases need to learn how to adapt their current policies or practices so that they can collaborate more effectively in community projects. Renard (1991a), for example, has suggested that donors need to incorporate small-scale initiatives and funding, be more flexible, take more long-term approaches, and include institutional strengthening for communities in their programs. In interviews, agency representatives mentioned repeatedly the need for education at the community level and for better interinstitutional communication among themselves and with the rural communities.

For interinstitutional collaboration to occur, participating agencies must develop new skills and techniques for working more closely with communities. Jamaica has been successful in its approach of including community concerns in the new parks being established (Island Resources Foundation, 1992). It has worked with existing NGOs and community groups, and has helped form new community organizations to act as local advisory committees for the parks. In the process, the park management staff has learned a great deal about how to approach community involvement and how it can help to strengthen community groups to become stronger partners in working for common goals.

What kinds of education are needed? Communities, and the agencies that can assist them, may need training and education in three broad categories: technical information, communication skills, and institutional strengthening. For example, communities need to know specifically what they want assistance with; they need to know whom to ask and how to ask for it; and they need the institutional strength to manage it effectively once they get it. And assistance agencies need to know when to give assistance, how to understand the community's request, and how to monitor progress.

Technical training in environmentally sound farming techniques is often identified as critical in community education programs conducted in buffer-zone areas. Notably, in case-study interviews, both the Jamaican and U.S. Government representatives identified community environmental education as an important activity for the buffer zone (rated third in frequency after stewardship and interinstitutional communication). Technical training in environmental issues is most important when it is identified as a need by the community itself. However, communities often are interested in environmentally sound techniques only when they can improve current practices (in the relatively short term) and when they improve or maintain current levels of production. Rural people are concerned about sustainability, for their children and grandchildren, but this is often a less urgent priority than immediate income and health.

Improved communication skills are needed by the communities and the agencies working with them so that they better understand each other and how they can work together. As has just been said, interinstitutional communication was listed second among the priority needs for management of the buffer zone. In addition, poor communication between assistance agencies and local communities was identified as a main threat to the buffer zone by the Jamaican Government and the international community. Communication training could include such topics as how to make effective presentations, how to communicate with farmers, how to write proposals, and how to contact and network with other institutions for establishing collaborative relationships.

Institutional strengthening is perhaps the most important need of community groups and local NGOs for greater cohesion and continuity. Leadership training is a key to fostering new leaders and to encouraging those whose leadership is already established. Training often seems to be concentrated on one dynamic person from a community whose charisma stands out in the group. Though this strategy is understandable when opportunities and funds are limited, it can also be detrimental.

85

Until others can catch up and begin making their own contributions to the development effort, the trained person may continue to take the lion's share of responsibility. Jealousies can occur, and the trained person may feel cut off from the group. As was observed in one of our study communities, there is a greater chance for "burnout" and stagnation in the group if advancement is occurring in such a skewed way. A good example of training is found in the Protected Areas Resource Conservation Project (the project that has established Jamaica's parks). The project has developed a team of trained people who understand and support each other. Because of training offered to this core group, more knowledge and responsibility are shared among a larger circle of people, thereby augmenting human resources and multiplying the flow of benefits to affected communities.

Other types of institutional strengthening that may be needed include a range of operational skills such as planning, proposal writing, and money management. The community planning aspect of our study seemed very successful. The community became more supportive of the Citizens Association; project ideas that had merely been discussed for years became formulated; and with a development plan, the community had a tool to begin searching for assistance to achieve its goals. We found that NGOs working with community groups have an important role to play in strengthening community organizations. As Renard (1991a) argued, they can often provide assistance in developing ideas into well-articulated proposals, and can also act as "brokers" to community groups by contributing technical and financial assistance, as well as institutional support for funded projects.

How should the education be conducted? According to many authors (e.g., Renard, 1991b; Ham, 1992; and Werner and Bower 1982), effective training and education programs are planned and implemented so that they (1) are relevant to the intended group, (2) focus on needs or issues identified by the target group, and (3) are implemented in a way that is conducive to learning and future application by affected populations. Any education or training program must be culturally appropriate so that it is relevant to the audience. Perhaps the best way to ensure this is to involve the community as much as possible in the design of the training. People are more likely to embrace training programs they feel are their own because they have greater confidence that their needs are being addressed by the training and that the most sensible logistics are being determined by those who know best--themselves.

86

A social learning atmosphere in which people learn together has a better chance for changing people's behavior (Friedmann, 1987). Therefore, the forum where education or training takes place should be conducive to people's expressing their ideas comfortably. In most cultures, this probably means small groups and informal settings, centrally and conveniently located.

As in any kind of training, appropriate examples should be used so that the audience can relate to them and understand the message. Generally, it is best to use familiar venues, formats, media, and materials. Drake (1991) offered several techniques for involving community members in education, including community maps, problem trees, group decision-making, public meetings, research teams, fact-finding missions, and popular theater. Her point is that training, particularly if it involves technical information, must be tailored to the needs, tastes, and abilities of the target group.

Practical training is important not only for more concrete understanding, but also to build experience and confidence. According to Bunch (1982), successful development starts with small projects and gradually builds on its own successes. Any tangible benefits from training programs, such as employment or opportunities for additional education, should be shared locally (Rowntree, 1992). Once initiated, benefits of the training should be shown as soon as possible in order to reinforce the perception among local people that improvement is within their grasp, and thereby encourage the process to continue.

Summary of Lessons Learned

In developing countries, rural people are most interested in conservation when they perceive it to be compatible with earning a livelihood. Interest in learning new techniques that are environmentally sound usually exists only to the extent that they will maintain or increase current levels of production. There also is an interest in learning about alternative income-generating activities that may or may not be natural-resource-based. Sustainability is a concern, though probably not an immediate priority.

Training and education are needed to bring communities and assistance agencies together and to foster collaboration between them. Through their community outreach programs, park-management agencies can and should assist local communities, but they are often limited in what they can do. Parks should facilitate community participation and interinstitutional collaboration without dominating the process. Creating a situation in which communities become too dependent on the park detracts from the development of the community's co-management capabilities and, in the long term, undermines sustainability.

All communities have leaders, and the leadership potential in communities should be evaluated and strengthened. Training for communities should help build local leadership and strengthen organizational and communication skills. With this audience there is a particular need for training in proposal writing, accounting, fund-raising, program design, and ways of implementing programs efficiently and inexpensively.

Donor and assistance agencies should not focus training on just one individual from a group but work with a subgroup, or a core of at least several people. This approach leads to a group that has shared experiences, allowing mutual support among its members. Otherwise, a small subset of trained people may be burdened with most of the work, increasing the chance for jealousy and burnout and decreasing the spread of the benefits from the training. It is difficult for a group or organization to develop and grow if access to knowledge is closed to all but a few people.

Donors also need education about how best to assist local groups and what "assistance" entails. These groups mainly need small amounts of money, long-term commitment for project development, and technical and moral support. It is best to start with small, feasible projects that are likely to bring success and slowly build to more complex projects, so that along the way the community can gain experience and increase its self-confidence.

There should be some kind of cohesive plan to work from so that projects do not overlap or bounce aimlessly to unrelated or ill-conceived goals. The community should follow some sort of planning process so that it (1) has an ideal or goal to work toward, (2) can get community input and a sense of agreement on this goal, and (3) can logically lay out small projects that in succession will lead to the goal. In this way, the community, rather than an outside agency, determines its own priorities and needs, thereby taking responsibility for its own development and greatly increasing the likelihood that sustainable courses of action will be found.

References

Barzetti, Valerie (ed.). 1993. *Parks and Progress: Protected Areas and Economic Development in Latin America and the Caribbean.* Gland, Switzerland, and Washington, D.C. World Conservation Union/Inter-American Development Bank.

Brandon, Katrina, and Michael Wells. 1992. "Planning for People and Parks: Design Dilemmas." *World Development*, vol. 20, no. 4. pp. 557-570.

Brown, Michael, *et al.* 1992. "Buffer Zone Management in Africa: Searching for Innovative Ways to Satisfy Human Needs and Conservation Objectives." Synthesis and discussion of a workshop in Queen Elizabeth National Park, Uganda, October 5-11, 1990. Washington, D.C. United States Agency for International Development.

Bunch, Roland. 1982. *Two Ears of Corn: A Guide to People-Centered Agricultural Improvement.* Oklahoma City. World Neighbors.

Csuti, Blair. 1991. "Conservation Corridors: Countering Habitat Fragmentation." In Wendy Hudson (ed.), *Landscape Linkages and Biodiversity.* Washington, D.C. Island Press.

Drake, Susan. 1991. "Local Participation in Ecotourism Projects." In Tensie Whelan (ed.), *Nature Tourism: Managing for the Environment.* Washington, D.C. Island Press. Chapter 7. pp.132-163.

Espeut, Peter. 1990. "An Economic Analysis of a Rural Jamaican Community." Mona, Jamaica. University of the West Indies, Consortium Graduate School of the Social Sciences. (unpublished master's thesis)

Friedmann, John. 1987. *Planning in the Public Domain: From Knowledge to Action.* Princeton, N.J. Princeton University Press.

Garrett, Keith. 1984. "The Relationship Between Adjacent Lands and Protected Areas: Issues of Concern for the Protected Area Manager." In Jeffrey McNeely and Kenton Miller (eds.), *National Parks, Conservation, and Development: The Role of Protected Areas in Sustaining Society.* Gland, Switzerland. International Union for the Conservation of Nature and Natural Resources. pp.65-71.

Geoghegan, Tighe. 1985. "Public Participation and Managed Areas in the Caribbean." *Parks*, vol. 10, no. 1. pp. 12-14.

Gorman, M.L. 1979. *Island Ecology.* London. Chapman and Hall.

Ham, Sam. 1992. *Environmental Interpretation: A Practical Guide for People with Big Ideas and Small Budgets*. Golden, Colo. North American Press.

Ham, Sam, David Sutherland, and James Barborak. 1989. "Role of Protected Areas in Environmental Education in Central America." *Journal of Interpretation*, vol. 13, no. 5. pp. 1-7.

Ham, Sam, David Sutherland, and Richard Meganck. 1993. "Applying Environmental Interpretation in Protected Areas in Developing Countries." *Environmental Conservation*, vol. 20, no. 3. pp. 232-242.

IUCN/MAB/UNESCO. 1979. *The Biosphere Reserve and its Relationship to Other Protected Areas*. Gland, Switzerland. International Union for the Conservation of Nature and Natural Resources.

Island Resources Foundation. 1992. "Evaluation Report of the Protected Areas Resources Conservation Project (PARC), Jamaica." Kingston, Jamaica. United States Agency for International Development.

Jacques, Mary Beth. 1986. "Participatory Environmental Planning in Central America; Case Study: The Rio Platano Biosphere Reserve, Honduras." Tufts University, Department of Urban and Environmental Policy. (unpublished master's thesis)

Lovejoy, Thomas E. 1984. "Biosphere Reserves: The Size Question." *Conservation, Science, and Society*, vol. I. Paris. UNESCO-UNEP. pp. 146-151.

MacFarland, Craig. 1984. "Relating the Biosphere Reserve to Other Protected Areas: Management Categories." *Conservation, Science, and Society*, vol. I. Paris. UNESCO-UNEP. pp. 196-203.

Machlis, Gary, and David Tichnell. 1985. *The State of the World's Parks: An International Assessment for Resource Management, Policy, and Research*. Boulder, Colo. Westview Press.

MacKinnon, John and Kathy, Graham Child, and Jim Thorsell (eds.). 1986. *Managing Protected Areas in the Tropics*. Cambridge, U.K. International Union for the Conservation of Nature and Natural Resources.

McLaughlin, William, Charles Black, and Peter O'Connell. 1992. "The Tweed Shire Tourism Strategy: Implications of a Local Tourism Planning Process." In P.J. Stanton (ed.), *The Benefits and Costs of Tourism*. Proceedings of a National Tourism Research Conference (East Perth, Australia, October 3-4, 1991).

McNeely, Jeffrey A. (ed.). 1993. *Parks for Life: Report of the IVth World Congress on National Parks and Protected Areas* (Caracas, Venezuela, February 10-21, 1992). Gland, Switzerland. World Conservation Union.

Norton, Bryan G., and Robert E. Ulanowicz. 1992. "Scale and Biodiversity Policy: A Hierarchical Approach." *Ambio*, vol. 21, no. 3. pp. 244-249.

Nietschmann, B. 1984. "Biosphere Reserves and Traditional Societies." *Conservation, Science, and Society*, vol. II. Paris. UNESCO-UNEP. pp. 499-508.

Renard, Yves. 1990. "Management of the Environment: Popular Participation and Community Responsibility." Paper presented at the Caribbean Studies Association XV Annual Conference (Santo Domingo, Dominican Republic, January 14-17, 1990). (unpublished)

Renard, Yves. 1991a. "Institutional Challenges for Community-based Management in the Caribbean." *Nature and Resources*, vol. 27, no. 4. pp. 4-9.

Renard, Yves. 1991b. "Strategies for Increasing Community Involvement in Ecotourism." Paper presented at the Caribbean Conference on Ecotourism (Belize, July 9-12, 1991). (unpublished)

Renard, Yves, and Leslie Hudson. 1992. "Overview and Symposium Paper for the Workshop on Community-Based Management of Protected Areas." Paper presented at the IVth World Congress on National Parks and Protected Areas, (Caracas, Venezuela, February 10-21, 1992).

Rocheleau, Dianne. 1991. "Participatory Research in Agroforestry: Learning from Experience and Expanding our Repertoire." *Agroforestry Systems*, vol. 15, no. 1. pp. 111-137.

Rowntree, Matthew. 1992. "Parks and Local Communities: Some Guidelines for Integration." Paper presented at the IVth World Congress on National Parks and Protected Areas (Caracas, Venezuela, February 10-21, 1992).

Saint Lucia. 1985. "People's Participation in Development and the Management of Natural Resources." Report on the Caribbean Regional Workshop (Vieux Fort, Saint Lucia, April 15-19, 1985). Caribbean Conference of Churches/Caribbean Conservation Association/ECNAMP/Government of Saint Lucia Forestry Division.

Thelen, K.D., and G.S. Child. 1984. "Biosphere Reserves and Rural Development." *Conservation, Science, and Society*, vol. II. Paris. UNESCO/UNEP. pp. 470-477.

von Droste zu Hulshoff, Bernd, and William P. Gregg, Jr. 1985. "Biosphere

Reserves: Demonstrating the Value of Conservation in Sustaining Society." *Parks*, vol. 10, no. 3. pp. 2-5.

Werner, David, and Bill Bower. 1982. *Helping Health Workers Learn: A Handbook of Methods, Aids and Ideas for Instructors at the Village Level.* Palo Alto, Cal. Hesperian Foundation.

Wind, Jan. 1991. *Effective Buffer Zones: Examples of Possible Buffer Zone Areas and Programs.* Proceedings of the Symposium on Rain Forest Protection and National Park Buffer Zone Development (Jakarta, Indonesia, February 7, 1991). Indonesian Nature Conservancy.

Wood, David, and Diane Walton Wood. 1990. *How to Plan a Conservation Education Program.* Washington, D.C. World Resources Institute/United States Fish and Wildlife Service.

Chapter 8

THE NEW REGIONAL PLANNING AND IMPLEMENTATION OF THE CONVENTION ON BIOLOGICAL DIVERSITY

Arturo Martínez

Introduction

During the negotiation of the Convention on Biological Diversity (CBD) the four points outlined in the Introduction of this volume were intensively discussed and supported. These four points--"Conservation as a Development Tool" (Articles 1 and 20(4)), "Consider the Neighbors" (Article 14), "Broaden the Development Agenda" (Article 8 (i)), and "Systems Thinking" (Article 10)--briefly summarize the new paradigm that establishes that without conservation of biodiversity, there is no development for future generations.

The importance given to this paradigm by both developed and developing countries is reflected in the speed with which they have endorsed the Convention, which is a binding intergovernmental instrument. It entered into force in December 1993, after having been signed in Rio in June 1992. More than 100 countries were already parties to the CBD when the first meeting of the Conference of the Parties was held in November of 1994, and its full implementation is now under way. An important facet of the CBD is the political realization that all human beings--whether from developed or developing countries--are responsible for the loss of biological diversity, though with differing degrees of responsibility. Another important contribution of the CBD is the provision of a basic standard for enhancing cooperation to fulfill its objectives.

The three objectives of the CBD are the conservation of biodiversity, the sustainable use of its components, and the fair and equitable sharing of the benefits derived from the utilization of genetic resources. On the basis of these objectives, the CBD recognizes first that conservation and sustainable use are closely interrelated. Second, it acknowledges the right of sovereign states to determine access to genetic resources and to share the benefits derived from their use. Third, it recognizes the expertise of local and indigenous communities in the conservation and sustainable use of biodiversity, in particular in agriculture, forestry, and fisheries.

In Agenda 21 and the CBD, there is no reference to operational units except for the concept of protected areas. However, the CBD objectives go beyond protected areas by referring to sustainable use of the components of biodiversity. So far there has been no attempt to define a portion of the earth's surface with some kind of common element such as a river basin or a coastal region where an integrated plan for conserving biodiversity is being developed. This is the reason why the new regional planning concept could be an integrated operation to help countries to develop national strategies for implementing the CBD. The purpose of this paper is to describe the aspects of the CBD that should be taken into account in defining the new regional planning model.

Activities Under the CBD

Articles 7, 8, 9, and 14 describe the activities that the parties need to carry out to comply with the objectives of the CBD. These articles are key to its implementation.

Article 7 deals with the identification and monitoring of the components of biodiversity. The process of identifying any living organism is a continuous basic inventory in support of any plan or program for conservation and sustainable use in any region. It is a straightforward, essential scientific action that should accompany any process of regional planning.

With regard to the other relevant point in Article 7, the need for monitoring, the CBD provides some technical guidance (Article 7(a)), leaving the complicated process of organizing an effective monitoring system to the countries. However, some general guidance must be developed to assist in the organization, management, and operation of a monitoring system. For example, the area where the system will be used needs to be defined. In this sense the new concept of a region as an integrated unit for action may facilitate the difficult process of monitoring. It is also important to remember that monitoring the components of biodiversity needs to have a framework of time and space. An ecophysiological experiment might be set up in which efforts would be made to define dimensions and variables in order to obtain predictable results. The definition of parameters is a key condition for an effective diagnosis; advanced technology is contributing to this important field of ecosystem management.

The same article recommends rather repetitively the identification of processes and categories of activities having significant adverse impacts (Article 7(c)). It may be that the negotiations uncovered some reason for identifying indirect socioeconomic activities resulting in deforestation, unsustainable agriculture, the drainage or filling of wetlands, unsustainable use of river basins and marine coastal areas, overfishing, pollution, and loss of biodiversity. Indirect adverse impacts can cause neighboring similar ecosystems to suffer from different adverse impacts.

Article 14 complements the recommendations of Article 7(c) by calling for action to minimize adverse impacts. It also encourages the conclusion of bilateral, regional, or multilateral arrangements to reduce activities that have a significant adverse effect on the biological diversity of other states or areas beyond the limits of national jurisdiction (Article 14(c)). Here the CBD provides a legal basis for considering the health of biodiversity in neighboring states or areas, as described in the Introduction.

Article 8, on *in-situ* conservation, is the key article of the CBD in this context, and the concept of new regional planning can assist in its implementation. This article considers that a protected-area system should not be established without taking into account the political, social, economic, and environmental aspects of the region. The new concept of integrated region can help in particular to implement the aspects mentioned in paragraphs (a) to (e) concerning the establishment and management of protected areas and their surroundings.

In Article 8(j), the parties agree that if the knowledge, innovations, and practices of indigenous and local communities are not respected, preserved, and maintained, humanity is losing experience, knowledge, and technology for conserving biodiversity. The provision in the CBD for improving the standard of living of these communities by making them partners in the benefits derived from the use of the genetic resources that they are continuously providing is a moral and a utilitarian recommendation. The CBD recognizes the moral debt that this generation owes to traditional and indigenous communities for their contribution to modern agriculture and medicine. In addition, there are utilitarian reasons to preserve and improve the living conditions of traditional and indigenous communities, since it is widely recognized that close collaboration with these communities will enhance the genetic diversity of crops and provide new pharmaceutical products to modern medicine. The CBD provides legal support to these still-marginal communities by introducing concern for their preservation into the international agenda.

Implementing Article 8(j) will not be easy. Perhaps, as is pointed out by Glowka *et al.* (1994), the first step might be to provide rights under national legislation to indigenous and local communities. Exchange of experiences and knowledge can help countries to consider seriously the conservation of traditional practices for future generations. Regional cooperation through the organization of seminars and workshops on political, legal, economic, and scientific aspects can assist governments in complying with Article 8(j).

Ex-situ conservation (Article 9) is a means of supporting actions to rehabilitate and restore degraded ecosystems (Article 8(f)), and to develop sustainable agriculture, forestry, and fisheries. Article 9 says specifically that measures to conserve genetic resources should preferably be taken in their country of origin, but very few developing countries have the facilities and human capacity to establish and maintain *ex-situ* facilities. This is one issue, together with identification of the components of biodiversity in Article 7, that needs fluid regional and global cooperation.

Sustainable Use of Biodiversity: Developing Incentive Measures

Perhaps the most progressive concept in the CBD is that conservation and development can be achieved through the sustainable use of the components of biodiversity. The concept of sustainability of biodiversity and the need for incentive measures were developed prior to the CBD in non-binding documents such as the *World Conservation Strategy* (IUCN *et al.*, 1980), *Our Common Future* (WCED, 1987), *Caring for the Earth* (IUCN, 1991), the *Global Biodiversity Strategy* (WRI *et al.*, 1992), and *Agenda 21* (UNCED, 1992).

During the CBD negotiations, these concepts were introduced in two articles: Article 10 on sustainable use of the components of biodiversity and Article 11 on incentive measures. Both provide an outline to be developed by each party to the CBD. One important element is the need for incentives and disincentives for developing sustainable agriculture, forestry, and fisheries.

The difficulty here is the still small number of economic incentives that will make the concept of sustainable use of natural resources attractive to the main actors. Public education (Article 13) using products from sustainable agriculture, forestry, and fisheries is one solution. At the same time policy-makers, particularly in the area of planning, have the obligation under the CBD to integrate conservation measures with socioeconomic aspects in the development of a protected-area system (Article 8 (c)).

Generating New Opportunities in Biodiversity Trade

One outcome of the CBD grants to sovereign states the rights and obligations regarding access to genetic resources (Article 15). This new responsibility of countries also creates opportunities for partnerships between countries with genetic resources and those with advanced sustainable use technologies (Article 16). Articles 15, 16, and 19 provide minimum standards for transactions in biodiversity trade (Downes, 1993). These standards are provided by Article 15, which outlines how to access genetic resources from the providers' point of view, and by Articles 16 and 19, which outline the kind of technology, including biotechnology, to be transferred and the requirements for such partnerships.

The provisions in Articles 15, 16, 18, and 19 should be linked to Articles 8, 9, and 11. A strategy to access genetic resources cannot be separated from a strategy for their conservation, either *in situ* or *ex situ*, and a consideration of the potential benefits expected from their use since these are one incentive for developing countries to conserve biodiversity.

Conclusions

The CBD enhances conservation by adding the concepts of sustainability and equitable sharing of the benefits derived from the use of genetic resources. In addition, the guidance for action recommended by Article 8(c) includes the regulation and management of biodiversity whether within or outside of protected areas.

This recommendation indicates that any political, social, or economic activity directly or indirectly related to biodiversity should be taken into consideration in developing national strategies, plans, and programs. This comprehensive approach of the CBD is a particular challenge for developing countries in which the major revenues are from agriculture, fisheries, and forestry and a high percentage of the population is involved in farming.

To pursue this approach and alleviate the loss of biodiversity, a process to define management tools is needed. The new regional planning concept, with clear and concrete objectives, can help in this. The main components to be taken into account in the planning are (1) human resources; (2) research and development of scientific and technical tools for the conservation and sustainable use of biodiversity; (3) institutional coordination through the development of synergy between different institutional capabilities; and (4) policies for information exchange, technology transfer, and regional and international cooperation. The planning itself should consider (1) indigenous knowledge and its value in the conservation and use of biodiversity (including traditional land management); (2) land tenure and land-use planning for conservation and appropriate bio-production, including forestry and agriculture; (3) ecological history and past land management; (4) identification of economic uses and potential market value of genetic resources (including plants, animals, and microorganisms); and (5) intellectual property regimes and their relation to the conservation and use of biodiversity.

Now that policy-makers have included the conservation of biodiversity as a priority in their agenda, the search for technically, socially, and economically viable means of implementing the CBD is the second step.

References

Downes, D.R. 1993. "New Diplomacy for the Biodiversity Trade: Biodiversity, Biotechnology and Intellectual Property in the Convention on Biological Diversity." *Touro Journal of Transnational Law*, Spring, vol. 4. pp. 1-46.

Glowka L., *et al*. 1994. *A Guide to the Convention on Biological Diversity*. Gland, Switzerland. World Conservation Union.

IUCN/UNEP/WWF. 1980. *World Conservation Strategy: Living Resource Conservation for Sustainable Development*. Gland, Switzerland. International Union for the Conservation of Nature and Natural Resources.

IUCN/UNEP/WWF. 1991. *Caring for the Earth: A Strategy for Sustainable Living*. Gland, Switzerland. World Conservation Union.

UNCED. 1993. *Agenda 21: Programme of Action for Sustainable Development*. New York. United Nations.

UNEP. 1992. *Convention on Biological Diversity*. Nairobi. United Nations Environment Programme.

WCED. 1987. *Our Common Future: The Report of the World Commission on Environment and Development*. New York. Oxford University Press.

WRI/IUCN/UNEP. 1992. *Global Biodiversity Strategy*. Washington, D.C. World Resources Institute.

Chapter 9

GREATER YELLOWSTONE TOMORROW: CHARTING A COURSE FOR A GREATER YELLOWSTONE FOREVER

Dennis Glick

Introduction

On a satellite image, Greater Yellowstone appears as a vast island of mountains and plateaus, rising up from the high plains where, except for Alaska, it forms one of the most extensive roadless tracts in the United States. The Ecosystem encompasses roughly 7,200,000 ha, including two national parks (Yellowstone and Grand Teton), portions of seven national forests, three National Wildlife Refuges, lands of the Bureau of Land Management, and state and private properties.

Characterized by largely pristine natural features, the region boasts the world's most extensive array of geysers and geothermal resources; some of the largest herds of elk, bison, and bighorn sheep in North America; over 300 species of birds (nearly half of the total species found in the entire United States); and several threatened or endangered plants and animals, ranging from the diminutive Yellow Spring Beauty to the majestic grizzly bear. Even more significant, Greater Yellowstone represents one of the largest essentially intact temperate-zone ecosystems on earth. It is a resource of national and international importance, and, not surprisingly, Yellowstone Park, at its core, was one of the first areas listed on the UNESCO registry of World Heritage Sites.

That Greater Yellowstone appears as an island of wildness isolated by encroaching development is cause for concern. Studies of archipelagoes cut off from the mainland by rising seas have documented the steady loss of species inevitably accompanying this fragmentation. In the western United States, investigations of the impact of the fragmentation of natural habitats found that nearly 40 populations of

101

mammals have disappeared from several national parks. Many of these sites are being whittled away as adjacent development converts them to wilderness islands awash in a sea of development.

With this in mind, close scrutiny of the satellite image of Greater Yellowstone is disturbing. To the west, a distinguishable straight line marks the boundary between Yellowstone Park and the Targhee National Forest (Figure 1). Over a billion board feet of timber has been cut in the Targhee since the 1960s. As cutting moves into increasingly fragile habitats, environmental impacts from both logging and road building increase erosion, destroy critical wildlife and fisheries habitat, and degrade scenic vistas.

Figure 1. Aerial View Showing the Boundary Between Yellowstone Park (left) and Targhee National Forest (right)

Photo: Tim Crawford, Greater Yellowstone Coalition.

The specter of widespread oil and gas exploration and development will continue to threaten the Park. Nearly five million acres of National Forest lands are under lease or lease application for oil and gas drilling. In the Bridger-Teton National Forest, for example, most of the available non-wilderness forest lands are proposed for leasing in the Final Forest Plan. Not only can oil and gas exploration and development affect wildlife and aesthetic values, they could cause irrevocable damage to the poorly understood subterranean plumbing responsible for Yellowstone's world-renowned geothermal features. New technologies often spawn new environmental problems. The cyanide-heap-leach processing of gold has sparked a dramatic increase in hard-rock mining in the West. The often destructive nature of mining and archaic mining laws have conspired to leave scars in Greater Yellowstone that may never heal. The McLaren mine, for example, located five miles upstream from Yellowstone's North Gate, is leaching a toxic heavy-metal soup that flows into the park. Off-site mining impacts such as road construction, increased human activity, power-line corridors, and the possibility of other mining-related disturbances exacerbate on-site impacts.

A host of other disturbances, though perhaps not as obvious as a clearcut or an oil derrick, erode the environmental stability of the area. The grazing of sheep and cattle, if not well managed, can degrade critical wildlife habitat such as riparian areas and winter range, increase erosion, and reduce water quality. Nearly two and a half million acres of federal land in Greater Yellowstone are open to sheep and cattle grazing. While impacts vary from site to site, there are numerous examples of direct competition between wildlife and livestock, In addition, concerns about depredation and a fear of the spread of brucellosis from bison to cattle have resulted in both the legal and illegal killing of wildlife. And there is stiff opposition to efforts to reintroduce or expand the range of predators such as wolves or grizzly bears from some in the livestock and outfitter industries.

Recreation-related impacts are of growing concern. An increase in recreational developments, such as the construction of the massive Grant Village and the rapid expansion of winter visitation in Yellowstone Park, could stress wildlife and increase mortality. The effects of other recreational pursuits such as off-road vehicle use and, in certain areas, non-motorized travel are poorly understood and merit analysis of their short- and long-term effects.

While many of these threats relate primarily to federal lands, the accelerating development of the "ecologically" strategic private lands is of equal concern. Though comprising less than a quarter of the region, private lands harbor key elements of the Ecosystem such as winter range,

103

migration corridors, and ecologically rich bottomlands. These areas also include important cultural and scenic values such as the farms and ranches that maintain the sense of wide-open spaces. Rampant subdividing, vacation-home construction, and other developments are cluttering these traditional landscapes and whittling away important habitats. For example, in Madison County, Montana, in the northeastern corner of the Ecosystem, over 85,000 acres have been subdivided into parcels of 200 acres or less.

The often-cited justification for this ill-conceived squandering of resources is that it will promote economic stability. Yet this argument flies in the face of reality. The rural economies of most counties of Greater Yellowstone have gone through a sweeping transition from resource extraction (timbering, mining, oil and gas development) to one more diversified and service-oriented. And it appears that this new economic base is firmly rooted in the natural amenities of the Ecosystem: clean air and water, good hunting and fishing, outdoor recreation, spectacular scenic vistas, untrammeled wilderness.

Just as resource utilization in the Ecosystem is often characterized by an insensitivity to the long-term health of the environment, a lack of coordination among resource managers is also a problem. Over twenty-five different federal and state agencies manage pieces of the Greater Yellowstone puzzle. Many have conflicting missions and management goals. Further complicating the situation are their varied procedures for collecting and analyzing data and determining appropriate resource-management practices.

The Greater Yellowstone Tomorrow Project

The mission of the Greater Yellowstone Coalition (GYC) is to ensure the long-term preservation of the Greater Yellowstone Ecosystem. To achieve this ambitious goal, the organization has carried out a multifaceted conservation program. This has included environmental awareness and education activities, the organization of grass-roots conservation efforts, the close monitoring of resource management and protection, and, when necessary, direct appeals of actions and plans of resource-management agencies that are considered undesirable.

In 1989, GYC launched its Greater Yellowstone Tomorrow (GYT) project, which is proactively planning for protection of the

Ecosystem. GYT was conceived when the Coalition Board of Directors discussed the idea of forging an "alternative vision" for the Greater Yellowstone based on a "solid understanding of Ecosystem functions, man's impact on these processes, and actions needed to assure long-term protection and restoration." The three principal goals of the project are:

(1) *To develop a blueprint for action* that clearly lays out the steps to long-term Ecosystem protection in Greater Yellowstone.

(2) *To organize an informed and motivated constituency* broad enough to ensure that recommended actions are carried out.

(3) *To serve as a catalyst* for the implementation of the blueprint by the year 2000.

Through Greater Yellowstone Tomorrow, the Coalition is designing an alternative future for the ecosystem, and identifying and implementing actions needed to make it a reality. The strategy to achieve these objectives features three major initiatives:

(1) *Profiling the Ecosystem.* The Environmental Profile analyzes the processes and components of Greater Yellowstone Ecosystem, including the unique relationships of humans within the Ecosystem. To illustrate the possible future of the region, the profile uses a series of maps and graphics that depict proposed development based on existing plans and growth trends.

(2) *Organizing a community outreach program.* Information collected for the Environmental Profile was widely disseminated in the communities of the Greater Yellowstone region. These community meetings also provided an opportunity for the GYT project staff to gain a better understanding of the concerns, aspirations, and plans of regional residents for their communities and surrounding areas.

(3) *Formulating a "blueprint" for action.* The Greater Yellowstone Tomorrow Blueprint for Action sets a new course for the protection and sound management of Greater Yellowstone's wildland and wildlife resources, geothermal features, open spaces, and outstanding scenic qualities. This component of the project also supports community efforts to plan for economic and environmental sustainability.

Project Status

(1) *Profiling the Ecosystem.* A requisite first step in solving the tough problems that cloud the future of Greater Yellowstone is the

building of a common base of understanding of the ecosystem and the threats to its well-being. This was the goal of the Tomorrow project's "Environmental Profile of the Greater Yellowstone Ecosystem," which was published and widely distributed in late 1991. The Profile represents the first-ever comprehensive analysis of the ecological and socioeconomic underpinnings of the Ecosystem. Based on the peer-reviewed writings of GYC's Science Council along with information generated from numerous other sources, the Profile graphically illustrates the significance of the Ecosystem and the world-class nature of its wildland resources. The Profile also includes a series of maps illustrating existing and proposed developments that affect the character or health of the region.

The findings of the Profile reinforced the position that Greater Yellowstone is unique in many ways, but that in particular it is of global importance for the essentially intact nature of its ecological components and processes. The Profile also underscores GYC's concern that if current development trends continue, we will see a steady erosion of the region's wild qualities, with direct effects on both the wild and the human inhabitants of the region.

A significant trend noted in the study is the regional transition from an economy based on the extraction of resources to one increasingly dependent on the protection of watersheds, scenery, and wildlife and wildland values. However, this new economy brings with it a new set of problems that must be anticipated and incorporated into the conservation efforts of both governmental and nongovernmental entities.

Finally, the Profile notes that throughout the Greater Yellowstone region, efforts are under way at the local, state, and federal levels to bridge the gap between conservation and development. These actions, through seldom coordinated, are nevertheless planting the seeds of sustainability.

The full Profile document was supplemented by an Executive Summary that crystallizes the major points of the report and several slide-show versions custom-tailored to different key audiences (see Community Outreach Program discussion below). A special issue of the *Journal of Conservation Biology* featured ten of the GYC Science Council's papers related to Greater Yellowstone. This was the first time that the *Journal* had published a series of articles taking a comprehensive (including socioeconomic) look at a geographic region.

County-specific socioeconomic profiles were developed for the twenty Greater Yellowstone counties. These are being used to help regional residents better understand their county-specific reality in regard to economic and demographic changes. They are proving useful to organizations within the region that are involved in economic and environmental sustainability. These profiles have also helped the Coalition to gain a better understanding of regional economic development issues.

The publication and dissemination of the complete Profile has laid the foundation for the drafting of a shared Blueprint for Ecosystem Protection by raising GYC's understanding of the ecological and economic underpinnings of the region, and the threats to their well-being. It has also provided a wealth of educational materials necessary for the nurturing of an informed constituency broad enough to ensure that Blueprint recommendations become a reality. Building this constituency and facilitating its involvement in creating the blueprint is the primary goal of the Tomorrow project's Community Outreach Program.

(2) *The Community Outreach Program.* The Community Outreach Program has attempted to raise the regional level of understanding and concern for the Greater Yellowstone Ecosystem, to stimulate local efforts to plan for environmental and economic sustainability, to incorporate the best thinking of regional residents into the development of the Blueprint, and to facilitate the creation of a community-generated vision for the future of the region.

The Community Outreach Program has taken the information gathered in the Environmental Profile to dozens of governmental and nongovernmental entities throughout Greater Yellowstone. These programs have provided an opportunity for GYC and a broad array of organizations to discuss their views and knowledge of the region. Indeed, this has been a two-way flow of information and understanding.

Some 27 different communities have been visited by Tomorrow project staff (Figure 2). Participants in Outreach Program activities have ranged from Chambers of Commerce to Conservation Districts, environmental groups to county commissioners, Rotary Clubs, state legislators, grazing associations, federal agencies, lumber-mill operators, and many others. The presentations have stimulated lively discussions on the future of the region. There has been a marked increase in grass-roots efforts to plan for community and county economic development and environmental protection. While it is difficult to prove whether the Community Outreach Program has been the catalyst for this activity, it has without doubt complemented this encouraging trend.

A questionnaire soliciting residents' desires and ideas on future economic development and environmental protection has been widely distributed. The information gleaned from these surveys was analyzed in an effort to determine whether there is some regional consensus on a desired future for Greater Yellowstone. The results of this and other similar surveys seem to indicate that there is indeed a broad appreciation for the wild character of the area and a strong desire to maintain this quality. If this assessment is correct, a major building block for crafting a shared vision for the future is already in place.

The GYT Outreach Program also served as a catalyst for a number of local efforts to create community-generated visions for the future. GYT staff introduced local residents to the "Successful Communities" process, which is organized by the Sonoran Institute of Tucson, Arizona. This consists of workshops that help towns to identify the natural and cultural amenities they most value and draft a shared strategy for protecting these values. The Sonoran Institute has organized a number of these workshops around the country and is generally perceived as an unbiased, neutral facilitator (in contrast to GYC, which is well known as an environmental advocacy group). Five communities in Greater Yellowstone participated in the Successful Communities program. In all cases a broad diversity of community residents were able to formulate development and conservation goals. The actual implementation of these plans has varied from town to town. But the program did demonstrate that even in the highly polarized environment of the Northern Rockies, finding common ground on environmental and development issues is possible.

(3) *Development of the GYT Blueprint for Ecosystem Protection.* The ultimate goal of the Tomorrow project is to chart a course for the long-term protection of the Ecosystem and to begin the process of carrying out these activities. The Blueprint is both articulating the route that needs to be followed and illustrating what the destination will look like once it is reached. The Blueprint represents the first comprehensive "game plan" for the overall protection of Greater Yellowstone that has been formulated with the input of regional residents. An effort by the federal agencies to develop their "vision" for the future of the region's national parks and forests failed primarily because of the lack of local support.

The Blueprint begins where the Profile ended--a description of the significance of the Greater Yellowstone Ecosystem. The bulk of the

Blueprint articulates what needs to be done at the local, state, and national levels in order to maintain and in some cases enhance the significant features. Recommendations are being formulated on administration, policy, law, on-the-ground management activities, research, education, economic and tax incentives, and other strategies. Some of these recommended actions will be illustrated with case studies (identified by the Community Outreach Program) to demonstrate their feasibility.

Figure 2. One of the 27 Different Communities Visited by Project Staff as Part of its Community Outreach Program

Photo: Tom Murphy

For each of the key resources of Greater Yellowstone--geothermal features, biodiversity, water resources, open space and scenic values, forests and range, wildlands--the following information is being developed:

a. State of the resource (based on the Profile and additional research)

b. Guiding principles (general overarching guidelines that should be taken into account when resource development or protection plans are being formulated)

c.   Recommendations (specific proposals for resource management and protection)
d.   Case studies (preferably from the region, to illustrate the types of activities that are being recommended)
e.   Implementation strategy (as a reality check, ideas for putting these recommendations into practice)

The Blueprint is being developed by GYC staff, with relevant information gathered from the communities, and from resource users and managers, information and advice gleaned from an advisory committee representing a broad range of perspectives and expertise, the GYC Science Council and Board, and many others. This research is uncovering many of the less obvious underlying causes of inappropriate resource-management activities in the region. It is also underscoring the broad range of perspectives on how these resources should be administered. A major challenge facing GYC on this aspect of the project has been coming to an internal consensus on the specific recommendations.

The Blueprint is expected to be published before the end of 1993. It will be widely distributed at both the regional and the national level. Plans call for a return to many of the communities visited during the Community Outreach Program. These meetings will provide a forum to discuss Blueprint recommendations, identify where community input was incorporated into the document, and launch collaborative efforts to implement recommended actions that address issues of common concern.

Conclusion

The Greater Yellowstone Tomorrow project achieved its dual goal of articulating a vision for the future of Greater Yellowstone and developing a Blueprint for Ecosystem Protection. Whether it will also raise the regional level of Ecosystem awareness and stimulated support for the implementation of Blueprint recommendations is yet to be determined.

More than just a plan or a strategy, the Tomorrow project is meant to be a vehicle for sociopolitical and economic change that is as dynamic and alive as Greater Yellowstone itself. The Tomorrow project has embodied the ecological makeup of this land, with varied components all interacting and making up a whole greater than the sum of its parts.

In a sense, the process being used to formulate the Blueprint is as important as the document itself. More than just awakening broad interest in the fate of the Ecosystem, GYT is attempting to stimulate a strong desire to follow through with the actions needed to guarantee that Greater Yellowstone Tomorrow's goals are fully achieved.

While directed by the Coalition, GYT has involved the participation of numerous individuals and organizations--undoubtedly one of the more important measurable outcomes of this planning process which will pay "dividends" far into the future as stakeholders are convinced of the value of their input into management decisions. Efforts are being made to ensure that the project is as interactive as possible; that is, an honest sharing of views and information involving numerous individuals and agencies--something easier said than done. While GYC is striving to produce a truly visionary blueprint, we want this to be a vision shared by many. Whether this goal will be fully achieved is impossible to predict at this time. But the blossoming of similar efforts at the local level throughout Greater Yellowstone is an encouraging sign. There is now nearly unanimous agreement that we need to plan proactively for the future. The GYT project is attempting to harness this energy.

Chapter 10

THE LA AMISTAD BIOSPHERE RESERVE

Juan José Castro, Manuel Ramírez,
Richard E. Saunier and Richard A. Meganck

Introduction

This paper describes the bases for organizing recent planning for the establishment and administration of the proposed La Amistad International Biosphere Reserve of Costa Rica and Panama. It discusses the successes and failures to date in the efforts to establish the Reserve, draws conclusions from these, and makes recommendations as to how the process might be used elsewhere.

Because of the uniqueness of the area and the international interest in binational conservation areas and biodiversity conservation through the use and implementation of landscape planning, the La Amistad International Parks (PILA) of Costa Rica and Panama as well as the proposed International Biosphere Reserve along their common border have often been discussed (Fábrega, 1993; Arias and Nations, 1993; WRI *et al.*, 1992; Associated Press, 1990; Torres, 1988; Torres *et al.*, 1987; Houseal *et al.*, 1985; Morales *et al.*, 1984). The core area of the proposed international biosphere reserve would consist of the currently existing La Amistad parks of both countries, Volcán Barú National Park in Panama, and the Chirripó National Park in Costa Rica. A number of adjacent indigenous territories, forest reserves, wildlife conservation areas, and protected watersheds represent the buffer zones and multiple-use areas.

Consisting of approximately 200,000 ha in each country, the PILA covers a majority of the Cordillera de Talamanca, a mountain range rising from near sea level to over 3,800 m. Because of its location and variation in altitude, the region contains nearly a dozen different Holdridge life zones in Costa Rica (OAS/CI, 1990), and the final proposal from Panama for its portion of the reserve will most certainly add to this total (Table 1).

This landscape dominates the region and forms a physical backbone that ties the two countries together. For millennia, this mountain range has provided a land bridge that even today allows the exchange of North and South American biota. It remains a refuge for a diverse flora and fauna, many of which are rare or endangered (Gómez, 1989; Alvarado, 1988). The high annual rainfall of between 2,000 and 7,000 mm, combined with the short and steep watersheds common to the region, creates both serious flood hazards and a potential for hydroelectric energy production. The National Electric Institute of Costa Rica (ICE) considers that the Sixaola River--which forms a portion of the border between the two countries--and its tributaries have 10 potential sites for hydroelectric projects in Costa Rica alone (OAS/CI, 1990). The two rivers in Panama that have the highest hydroelectric potential, the Teribe and the Changuinola, arise in this same area (MIPPE, 1992). Likewise, the occurrence of coal (Chuprine, 1993), gold (Houseal *et al.*, 1985), petroleum (Medina, 1991), and "available" land (Imbach and Alvarado, 1990; ISTI, 1980) is at the same time problematical and possibly auspicious.

Talamanca has contained human occupants for thousands of years, and for Costa Rica it is the area that holds the largest indigenous populations remaining in the country--the largest of which are the Bribrí and the Cabecar, which together amount to a population of nearly 12,000. Panama also has a number of indigenous communities within the region: 60,000 Guaymí (divided into the Ngobe and the Buglere); the Teribe (or Naso), who number 5,000; and a population of Bribrí of unknown size that arrived in Panama from Costa Rica in 1960.

The Proposed La Amistad International Biosphere Reserve

In May of 1982, the governments of Costa Rica and Panama signed an agreement to create the La Amistad International Park. Costa Rica legally established its sector of the park in February of 1982 and the Panamanian sector followed in 1988. However, the history of the proposal to establish an international conservation area along this border goes back to 1974 and the First Central American Meeting for the Conservation of Natural and Cultural Resources.

114

Sponsored by FAO, IUCN, UNESCO, and the OAS, the encounter called for the establishment of international parks along national borders (IUCN, 1976).

Table 1. Major Holdridge life Zones in the Talamanca Massive of Panama and Costa Rica

- Tropical Moist Forest

- Tropical Wet Forest

- Tropical Wet Forest transition to Premontane Forest

- Premontane Wet Forest

- Premontane Wet Forest transition to Tropical Forest

- Premontane Wet Forest transition to Rain Forest

- Premontane Rain Forest

- Lower Montane Wet Forest

- Lower Montane Rain Forest

- Montane Rain Forest

- Subalpine Rain Páramo

- Lower Montane Moist Forest (Panama)

- Montane Wet Forest (Panama)

That meeting was followed by historic encounters between the presidents of Costa Rica and Panama in 1979 and 1982 in which they

115

instituted a binational commission on natural resources and instructed their respective natural resource management agencies to initiate joint planning and management of the wildlands along their common border (Gobierno de Costa Rica/Gobierno de Panamá, 1979). Each of these meetings emphasized two important arguments for the creation of such international parks: to conserve the natural and culture patrimony of a wider region and to serve as models for peace and friendship between neighboring countries.

Although progress has been slow, the proposal is being actively studied under the combined sponsorship of the two governments, the OAS, and Conservation International. Many other activities related to the proposal are also under way. These vary by country but include efforts by IUCN, the European Community, and UNEP.

(1) *The La Amistad Biosphere Reserve/Costa Rica.* The Government of Costa Rica formally organized the management of areas surrounding its portion of the PILA when it declared a 612,570 ha biosphere reserve covering most of its portion of the Talamanca range (the RBA/CR). Made up of 15 different units, the reserve includes two national parks, two biological reserves, a forest reserve, a wildlife reserve, a protected watershed, seven indigenous reserves, and a botanical garden.[1] UNESCO declared the area a Biosphere Reserve in 1982, and in 1983 it was accepted as a World Heritage Site.

In 1988, because of mounting management problems and conflicts among the many agencies operating within the RBA/CR, a coordinating commission (CCRBA) of representatives of the major institutions having jurisdiction over land use in that area was created (CI, 1988). The commission was to be presided over by the Minister of Natural Resources, Energy, and Mines and included as members the directors of the other two public institutions controlling lands located within the Biosphere Reserve (the National Park Service and the Forestry General Directorate), the National Parks Foundation, the Executive Director of the National Commission of Indigenous Affairs, the Resident Director of the Organization of Tropical Studies, and the CCRBA General

---

[1]La Amistad International Park (Costa Rican Sector), Chirripó National Park, the Hitoy Biological Reserve, the Barbilla Biological Reserve, the Río Macho Forestry Reserve, the Tapanti Wildlife Reserve, the Las Tablas Protective Zone, and the indigenous reserves of Ujurras, Salitre, Cabegra, Talamanca, Tayní, Telire, Chirripó and the Wilson Botanical Garden.

Coordinator. Funding for the General Coordinator and additional staff and operating expenses to guide the implementation of the programs and projects came from the proceeds of a five-year debt-for-nature swap coordinated by Conservation International and the Central Bank (CI, 1988). Despite the creation of the CCRBA, problems and potential threats to the PILA continued to increase. As a consequence, in 1989, the Government of Costa Rica requested that the OAS and CI help to formulate an institutional development strategy for the CCRBA. It did so in part because the threats were by no means limited to private decisions and activities. During the analyses for the development of this strategy, for example, 33 major actual or proposed investment projects of various government sectoral agencies were found that had previously been unknown to the managers and administration of the Reserve.

The institutional strategy for the RBA was developed in late 1989 (OAS/CI, 1990), and the first set of development proposals tied to this strategy was prepared and presented to the donor community in late 1990 (CI/OAS, n.d.). Although the formulation of the strategy took less than six months and required no information or data beyond what already existed, it facilitated the design of management plans and identified development priorities. The process emphasized integrated regional planning, sought the leadership of the Ministry of National Planning and Economic Policy (MIDEPLAN), and promoted a number of meetings between public institutions and with private groups and individuals.

Because of its regional landscape focus, the strategy and its projects are recognized as central to development efforts throughout the Talamanca region. The package of proposals presented to donor agencies sought to secure indigenous people's land rights, help solve specific problems of communities located within the Biosphere Reserve, and compensate landowners for expropriated land in the reserve's core area. In consultation with the region's agroindustries and inhabitants, agricultural and forestry policies to improve land-use practices were formulated and recommendations for environmental-impact analyses of a number of development projects within the RBA/CR were made.

Consultations on a continuing basis with local governments, the private sector, national and international NGOs, and indigenous groups are also mandated by the strategy. And, because of the nature of the development activities and the potentially binational character of the project, the use of mediation as the accepted methodology for solving land-use conflicts was and is a major objective.

The integrated nature of the strategy and its vision of consensus building at the local level have helped it to secure funding from international donors. As of 1992 Sweden, Holland, the Global Environmental Facility, the MacArthur Foundation, and the joint efforts of CI and the McDonald's Corporation and the OAS together with UNEP have brought in some US$12 million for work in the RBA/CR.

In addition to prescribing how the objectives of these proposals could be met, the strategy and its process of project formulation met three other important objectives designed to provide order to the management and administration of the Biosphere Reserve. First, it paved the way for coordinating activities with MIDEPLAN and the three regional offices that have jurisdiction over development planning in the area of the reserve. Second, it helped the numerous agencies with activities in the region to recognize both the broader regional context of "sustainable development" and, within that, the need for biodiversity conservation outside, as well as within, the core areas. And, third, it laid out an alternative institutional structure beyond short-term modifications within the CCRBA itself.

This alternative institutional structure was offered because it was felt that conditions would soon demand a structure different from that of the CCRBA to administer the rich variety of resources extant in the landscape and to coordinate and cooperate with the more than 100 private and public agencies and formal groups active in Talamanca. Under this alternative the CCRBA would evolve from focusing almost exclusively on protection of the RBA/CR core areas to having a more broadly based mandate somewhat equivalent to that of a "regional authority" charged with the sustainable development of the Talamanca Landscape. The direction of the "authority" would be rotated among the major actors within the Biosphere Reserve, and additional public and private institutions of both national and local jurisdiction would become members of the Commission as interest in the reserve grew. As a matter of fact, this process of evolution is under way and has led to many of the functions of CCRBA being taken over by Iriria Tsochok, a private foundation committed to sustainable development in Talamanca (*Boletín Talamanca*, 1992).

(2) *The La Amistad Biosphere Reserve/Panama*. Because of differences in policies, government priorities, and procedures, activities to establish the La Amistad International Park and biosphere reserve in Panama were initiated later than those in Costa Rica and proceeded under

118

a different format. In addition, much more of the area of PILA/Panama was privately held, and negotiations on acquiring these lands postponed establishment of the International Park until early 1988 (Alvarado, 1988).

The Panama sector of the La Amistad International Park is managed by INRENARE (a public natural-resource-management agency) with support from ANCON, an environmental NGO. In 1989 the OAS and CI were requested by the Government of Panama to help support the establishment of its portion of an eventual "La Amistad International Biosphere Reserve."

Under the auspices of the Ministry of Planning and Economic Policy (MIPPE), the OAS, CI, and all major stakeholders were invited to attend a series of meetings in which the geographical coverage and institutional makeup of the proposed biosphere reserve were discussed. The results of these meetings were put into one proposal, which is currently being commented on by the public and private agencies in Panama for later submission to UNESCO for official recognition as a Biosphere Reserve, and a strategy has been drafted for submission to Government so that national- and international-level management activities can be initiated.

As proposed, the future biosphere reserve in Panama (RBA/Panama) consists of parts of the provinces of Bocas del Toro and Chiriquí and includes the La Amistad International Park, the area of the proposed Teribe Indigenous Reserve, Volcán Barú National Park, the Palo Seco Watershed Protection Forest, the area of the Guaymí indigenous territory, the Islas Bastimento Marine Park, and the Fortuna Forest Reserve.

Many of the problems confronted in establishing and managing the RBA/Panama are similar to those found in Costa Rica. One such problem was the conflict created by the granting of a concession to Texaco to explore for petroleum in Bocas del Toro--an area that covers much of the proposed biosphere reserve and portions of the PILA (Medina, 1991). Another is the initiation of a road through the Volcán Barú National Park which would help advance the agricultural frontier into the Park as well as to allow access to privately held areas.[2] Binational meetings were held to exchange experiences and ideas both on

---

[2] Letter from the Panama Audubon Society to the Public Works Commission of the Legislative Assembly objecting to the "Proyecto de Ley No. 30: Construcción de Carretera Nueva entre Boquete y Cerro Punta, Provincia de Chiriquí."

these problems and on those revolving around fund-raising, media coverage, and binational cooperation.

Other conflicts have been brought into the discussion and a more productive dialogue seems to have been initiated. Previously, as a result of national debate surrounding the proposed Guaymí District, the Guaymí General Congress had vigorously opposed any studies or execution of projects in the area of the proposed district, including that of creating a biosphere reserve, and the establishment of the La Amistad International Park. After consultations with representatives of this group, a formula was worked out for their full participation in the discussions on the proposed surface coverage, makeup, and administration of the RBA/Panama.

Despite the similarities of objectives and process, the work in Panama has been different because the RBA/Panama does not yet exist. As a consequence, a major objective of the effort was to make the establishment of the biosphere a reality. The overall objective, however, has not been forgotten: to bring the organizational and management status of the future biosphere reserve up to that of the Costa Rica portion so that the area along both sides of the border may be administered with coordinated objectives, similar criteria and management methods, and a comparable level of investment activity.

Conclusions

Several years of work in the Talamanca region with the governments of Costa Rica and Panama and their institutions and people have highlighted a number of considerations that must be accounted for when undertaking such a planning effort. Change, information flow, political will, and financing are four of the more important of these.

(1) *Change.* Large-scale physical change regularly occurs within the Talamanca region. For example, on April 22, 1991, a strong earthquake shook the eastern slope of Talamanca triggering landslides, creation of unstable debris dams, flooding, loss of infrastructure (Figures 1 and 2), injury, loss of life, and forced migration into the more sparsely occupied areas of the region by a significant portion of the local population (CRERT, 1991). This earthquake was not an isolated event. Talamanca lies at the confluence of the Cocos, Caribbean, and Nazca plates, and as a result of their movement the region has averaged a major

earthquake every 2.25 years in the three and a quarter centuries since local records have been kept. All of the more recent events have been accompanied by the loss of housing, infrastructure, services, and jobs. And all have stimulated human migrations throughout the area of the proposed biosphere reserve. Houseal and Weber (1989) have described the pressures leading to other such changes, all of which have threatened conservation activities in Talamanca. These include the construction of hydroelectric dams, oil and gas pipelines, roads, transmission corridors, and refineries as well as the activities of ranching, agricultural plantations, logging, and mining.

(2) *Information flow.* Involving local people and institutions in all phases of the planning of natural resources is vital to the survival of protected areas, development in their buffer zones, and the conservation of biodiversity outside of those "gates." Keeping NGOs, the local press, community groups, and schools abreast of the progress in planning and implementation helps to avoid criticism based on incomplete or false information. This latter point is particularly important if financing agencies are to get the complete picture of a project's impact and not a partial or negative view. A core of informed and involved people at the local level is excellent insurance for a project's survival. Looking at a "landscape" for its integrative and scientific values is only one way of seeing the problems of biodiversity conservation. Another is its value in identifying the pool of potentially conflictive decision-makers who must somehow become involved in a search for consensus on what the "best" decisions are.

(3) *Political will.* A lack of political will is often cited as the cause of planning failure. The planning efforts in La Amistad were fortunate, however, since if the creation of the La Amistad International Park and the La Amistad Biosphere Reserve had anything in its favor, it was sustained "political will" at the highest levels of government in both Costa Rica and Panama. In addition to the presidential declarations and sectoral agreements signed by the respective ministers, six binational technical commissions were established and are still functioning: health, agriculture and animal husbandry, natural resources, commerce and industry, public works and transportation, and municipalities. Interest on the part of presidents, however, does not necessarily mean a smooth process of planning. Despite this "political will," interagency conflicts will remain and these conflicts must be identified and considered if not resolved if a plan is to be successful.

Figures 1 and 2. Results of the April 22, 1991, Earthquake in the Bocas del Toro Region of Panama

Photos: Juan José Castro

122

(4) *Financing*. Efforts by numerous interested parties to gain required financing for the establishment and management of the RBA have been relatively successful.   However, despite the existence of a well-studied integrated strategy and a list of project proposals that have been studied in detail, funding these proposals remains difficult.   For better or worse, all donor institutions have their own agendas and ideas of what needs to be done and these may not fit a local strategy created to solve local problems.   Funding groups also have their own boards of directors, constituencies, donors, and interests. Finding common ground between these and the local users of the landscape remains a difficult task.

Outlook

The work to design the institutional, administrative, and management strategies and to secure funding for the development projects necessary to support the process of "sustainable development" in Talamanca is not finished. Nevertheless, several important lessons have been learned that can be applied elsewhere. They include lessons on the following topics:

(1) *Peace parks*. International protected areas along borders contribute to reducing border tensions and issues of access by rural inhabitants to resources. Commonalities in management problems on both sides of the border may eventually require a binational approach to long-term management of these protected areas and the surrounding buffer or multiple use areas.

(2) *Planning as a process*. A coordinating commission is often a necessity at the outset of the planning process in order to reduce interagency competition for the control of resources, to involve local people, and to serve as a centralized authority for the receipt and distribution of technical assistance and project development funds. But planning cannot be done by a committee. Iteration must be a part of any participatory planning process so that the objectives can become focused.

(3) *Financing*. A foundation may be a valuable mechanism for coordinating and stabilizing financing planning and management. The next logical step is that national and local foundations active in Talamanca form a coalition or consortium in order to coordinate their activities, as a means of facilitating long-term financial stability of the entire RBA.

(4) *The reality of interagency conflicts.* High-level political support is fundamental for moving the concept of an international park and overcoming the tendency of sectoral agencies to subdivide park planning and management functions into areas covered by each specific mandate.

(5) *Conservation outside the gates.* Protection of core areas and the concept of biodiversity conservation in La Amistad have positively affected the management of adjacent areas.

(6) *Using the available data.* The collection of a vast amount of new data is not necessarily required to prepare an initial management strategy. The important thing is to establish the reserve, design a draft management strategy, and *then* begin to refine it with new data, more sophisticated strategies, etc.

References

Alvarado, R.H. 1988. *Resumen de Información Básica sobre el Parque Internacional La Amistad.* Bocas del Toro, Panama. Instituto Nacional de Recursos Naturales Renovables, Dirección Regional No. 1. (mimeo.)

Arias, O., and J.D. Nations. 1992. "A Call for Central American Peace Parks." In Sheldon Annis and Contributors, *Poverty, Natural Resources, and Public Policy in Central America.* Washington, D.C. Overseas Development Council.

Associated Press. 1990. "Central American 'Peace Parks' Have Dual Mission." *The Washington Post*, Friday, November 23.

Barrera, I. 1992. "Informe Preliminar de la Tercera Reunión de Consulta sobre la Propuesta Reserva de la Biósfera La Amistad en Panama." Ciudad de Panama. Gobierno de Panama. (unpublished)

Blutstein, H.I., *et al.* 1970. *Area Handbook for Costa Rica.* Washington, D.C. American University, Foreign Area Studies (distributed by U.S. Government Printing Office).

Boletín Talamanca. Reserva de la Biosfera La Amistad. "Fundación Iriria Tsochok" (editorial). San José, Costa Rica. Fundación para la Defensa de la Tierra.

Chuprine, A. 1993. "La Explotación del Carbón Mineral en Talamanca." *Boletín Talamanca*, no. 7. San José, Costa Rica. Fundación para la Defensa de la Tierra.

CI. 1988. *Proceso de Coordinación Integral y Acciones Requeridas para el Manejo de la Reserva de la Biósfera de La Amistad.* Documento sometido al Ministerio de Recursos Naturales, Energia y Minas de Costa Rica. Setiembre. Washington, D.C. Conservación Internacional. (mimeo.)

CI/OAS. n. d. *Strategy for the Institutional Development of La Amistad Biosphere Reserve: A Summary.* Washington, D.C. Conservation International.

Costa Rica Earthquake Reconnaissance Team. 1991. "Costa Rica Earthquake of April 22, 1991, Reconnaissance Report." *Earthquake Spectra* (Supplement B to vol. 7). Oakland, Calif. Earthquake Engineering Research Institute.

Fábrega, L.C. 1993. "Estrategia para la Formulación e Implementación de Políticas para el Ordenamiento Ambiental de la Región de La Amistad, Panama." Document presented to the OAS meeting with Governments and donors, Washington, D.C., November 23 and 24, 1993.

Gobierno de Costa Rica/Gobierno de Panamá. 1979. *Declaración de Guabito, 3 de marzo. Declaración Conjunta sobre un Parque de la Amistad.* Signatarios: Lic. Rodrigo Carazo, Presidente de Costa Rica; Dr. Aristides Royo, Presidente de Panama. San José/Ciudad de Panamá.

Gómez, Luis D. 1989. *Unidades Naturales y Uso Actual de los Ecosistemas, de Recursos Naturales, Beneficios Potenciales en la Región de Talamanca-Amistad.* Consultoría para la OEA. San Jose, Costa Rica.

Houseal, B., *et al.* 1985. "Indigenous Cultures and Protected Areas in Central America." *Cultural Survival*, March.

Houseal, B., and R. Weber. 1989. "Biosphere Reserves and the Conservation of Traditional Land Use Systems of Indigenous Populations in Central America." In Gregg, Krugman, and Wood (eds.), *Fourth World Wilderness Congress*. Estes Park, Colo. U.S. Department of the Interior, National Park Service.

Hurtado de Mendoza, L. 1987. "Patrones Prehistóricos de Uso de la Tierra en los Bosques Tropicales de Costa Rica." Turrialba, Costa Rica. CATIE. *Chasqui*, no. 13. pp. 4-15.

Imbach, A., and R. Alvarado. 1990. *Estrategia Regional para el Desarrollo Sostenible de Bocas del Toro, Panama.* San José, Costa Rica. Central American Office, World Conservation Union.

Medina, C.C. 1991. "Se Acerca el Terremoto Ecológico: Incertidumbre Reina por Exploraciones de la Texaco en Bocas del Toro." *La Prensa*, Panama, 29 de julio.

MIPPE. 1992. "Marco de Referencia y Características Generales del Area Reserva de la Biósfera La Amistad Sector Panama." Ciudad de Panama. Gobierno de Panama. (unpublished)

MIRENEM/CI. 1989. *Plan de Acciones Inmediatas para el Manejo de la Reserva de la Biósfera La Amistad.* Paper presented to the II Taller Interinstitucional para la Planificación Integrada de La Amistad (Sarapiquí, Costa Rica, October).

Morales, R., J. Barborak, and C. MacFarland. 1984. "Planning and Managing a Multi-Component, Multi-Category International Biosphere Reserve: The Case of the La Amistad/Talamanca Range/Bocas de Toro Wildlands Complex of Costa Rica and Panama." Paper presented to the First International Biosphere Reserve Congress (Minsk, Byelorussia, U.S.S.R., 26 September to 2 October 1983).

OAS/CI. 1990. *Estrategia para el Desarrollo Institucional de la Reserva de la Biósfera "La Amistad."* A report to the Government of Costa Rica. San José, Costa Rica. MIRENEM/MIDEPLAN.

Rodríguez, N. 1992. "10 años: La Reserva de la Biósfera La Amistad." *Boletín Informativo Talamanca*, no. 4. San José, Costa Rica. Fundación para la Defensa de la Tierra.

Torres, H. 1987. "La Amistad Biosphere Reserve: Towards Sustainable Development." Turrialba, Costa Rica. CATIE/DRNR. (mimeo.)

UICN. 1976. *Actas de la Reunión Centroamericana sobre Manejo de Recursos Naturales y Culturales.* Morges, Switzerland. Unión Internacional para la Conservación de la Naturaleza y los Recursos Naturales. (Publ. Nueva Serie #36, 8.1.)

WRI/IUCN/UNEP. 1992. *Global Biodiversity Strategy.* Washington, D.C. World Resources Institute.

Chapter 11

COMMUNITIES, PARKS, AND REGIONAL PLANNING: A CO-MANAGEMENT STRATEGY BASED ON THE ZIMBABWEAN EXPERIENCE

Simon C. Metcalfe

Historical Background

A "community" in pre-colonial Zimbabwe consisted of a hierarchy of land communities nesting one within the other and with membership depending on acceptance by traditional authority at each level of authority. Common pool resources such as wildlife, grazing, firewood, and water were regulated within this structure (Holleman, 1966). While population densities were far less and fragmentation of habitat hardly a matter of great anxiety in the nineteenth century, Cousins (1987) states that the land-tenure system functioned as a mechanism of social control.

Interventions by the European colonial powers in the twentieth century in Africa had a radical impact on traditional land-tenure systems. Nations were established that cross-cut cultural and natural systems. Statutory laws were promulgated that alienated local people from land, grazing, forest, and wildlife resources. Rural people lost access to wildlands as protected areas were established and also lost legal access to wildlife on their own land. The appropriation by the state of natural resources generally led to the emergence of elements of an "open access" system, with individual entrepreneurship invading the commons as a collective sense of proprietorship was lost (Murphree and Cumming, 1990).

The Post-Colonial Dilemma

The independent states of sub-Saharan Africa have largely attempted to maintain the principle of state control of the wildlife estate.

In doing so they have served the tenets of conventional Western wildlife conservation and learnt little from the rural development experiences occurring all around the parks. Consequently, the parks and the park management became irrelevant to the local development effort. It is axiomatic that a management system that depends on external sanctions and incentives for success will collapse unless they are maintained. It would be a fair appraisal to state that areas in rural Africa protected by conventional law-enforcement methods have failed, as species become increasingly threatened and habitat isolated.

Many factors--population growth, poverty, corruption, and a lack of representation, viable local market economies, and good planning--combine with weak enforcement to contribute to the fragmentation of ecosystems around protected areas. If these islands were closely linked to local land-use planning, they could contribute to local development and might greatly enhance local appreciation of the value of biodiversity.

The concerns raised by conservation biologists regarding minimum viable areas for maintaining species diversity indicate that many parks are not self-sufficient. Protected areas are inadequate for the preservation of many large mammals and predators, as the habitat is insufficiently stable to protect biological processes and species adequately (Wilcox, 1980; Soulé, 1885; Shaffer, 1987; Western, 1989; Cumming, 1990).

Finally, most wildlife and its habitat actually exist outside of protected areas where the policy of state proprietorship in African savanna areas has nullified the potential value wildlife could have on communal and private land.

Empowering Local Management

The fortress mentality inherent in constantly defending parks in a losing battle against rural development led Zimbabwean ecologists to rethink wildlife management policy. It was noted that as long as all wildlife remained in the realm of the state, the public--private or communal--could not invest in it. Unless the public was granted access to wildlife there was no possibility of a multispecies production system approach to land use. Unless some complementarity exists between the protected and communal land, the "hard edge" approach continues, with increasing conflict over land use and management and regional planning.

128

With the Parks and Wildlife Act of 1975 the Zimbabwe Government, as the responsible authority, reconciled this conflict by granting the right to manage and administer wildlife ("appropriate authority") to landowners (private) and landholders (communal). The results were initially dramatic in the private sector, where land allocated to wildlife has expanded rapidly, competing with and complementing cattle-based range management systems (Child, 1991). In the communal sector the obvious difficulties inherent in common-pool resource management of a mobile (fugitive) resource have been addressed through the CAMPFIRE policy, now an integral part of the National Conservation Strategy.

In Zimbabwe it is the communal areas that largely surround the protected areas, and consequently it largely depends on the Department of National Parks and Wildlife Management and CAMPFIRE to reconcile parks and communities within a wider regional plan.

Managing the Communal Wildlife Areas

It has become clear in the CAMPFIRE program that to achieve a positive co-management structure three main stakeholders have to settle on an effective institutional framework and collaborate closely: the communities, their local authorities (councils), and the Ministry of Environment (parks, forests, and natural resources agencies). The communities are the primary stakeholders, and the environment agency is a technical support agency and arbitrator. The local authority is the lowest level of formal statutory accountability, and the only one to which statutory law can delegate powers.

This raises the vital issue of accountability between local authority and communities. Are the people accountable to the council or vice versa? Which way does democracy actually work? Are the people shareholders or labor? In response, the CAMPFIRE program has established a set of principles to guide the relationship between local councils and people. These principles attempt to avoid an unfair bureaucratic tax on the wildlife resource that domestic resources (livestock) do not have to suffer. They include the following (Murphree, 1991):

(1) Effective management of wildlife is best achieved by giving it focused value for those who live with it.

(2)   Differential inputs may result in differential outputs.

(3)   There must be a positive correlation between quality of management and the magnitude of benefit.

(4)   The unit of proprietorship should be the unit of production, management, and benefit.

(5)   The unit of proprietorship should be as small as practicable, within ecological and sociopolitical constraints.

The CAMPFIRE program cannot claim to have achieved its objectives, but can claim to be establishing the framework for developing institutional capacity in the local community for managing wildlife resources. That capacity, within acceptable community organization, will serve the management of natural resources in a holistic way as much as the single resource of wildlife.   The most positive way to educate a community on the importance of the natural processes of the ecosystem is to first empower them with responsibility for its costs and rents. The CAMPFIRE program argues strongly in favor of sustained use as the springboard for large-mammal diversity integration into communal land-use practices.   Such use outside a protected area is effectively subsidized by the preservationist approach of the protected zone. The park may be perceived as an eco-bank supplying interest in the form of a renewable supply of wild animals.   The softening of the "hard edge" between zones has always been a goal of buffer-zone approaches, but too often the relationship between people and park has been asymmetrical and not a genuine meeting of land uses and authorities (Brown, 1991).

People, Wildlife, and Property

Unlike crops and domestic livestock, wildlife is a common-pool resource like rivers, grazing lands, and forest areas.   Since it is mobile, communities need to know their boundaries and form collaborative associations with their neighbors. This is particularly necessary with large mammals and predators whose range is greater than any one basic CAMPFIRE unit.

By definition, common property resources are ones from which it is difficult to exclude interloping appropriators.   Privatization of the African rangelands is often not feasible, while state control has proved inadequate. A successful approach to this commons dilemma may be found in complementary and compatible relationships between the

130

resource, the technology for its exploitation, the property-rights regime and the larger set of institutional arrangements (Berkes, 1989). In cases of communities and their relations to protected areas, cooperative management arrangements (co-management) are needed, involving the sharing of power between governments and local communities. On communal land itself a common property-management system is implied.

Ostrom (1990) argues for the necessity of a set of design principles that have been illustrated by examples of long-enduring common pool resource (CPR) institutions.

(1) *Clearly defined boundaries*. Individuals and households who have rights to withdraw resource units from the CPR must be clearly defined, as must the boundaries of the CPR itself.

(2) *Congruence between appropriation and provision rules and local conditions*. Appropriation rules restricting time, place, technology, and/or quantity of resource units are related to local conditions and to provision rules requiring labor, material, and/or money.

(3) *Collective choice arrangements*. Most individuals affected by the operational rules can participate in modifying them.

(4) *Monitoring*. Monitors, who actively audit CPR conditions and appropriator behavior, are accountable to the appropriators or are the appropriators.

(5) *Graduated sanctions*. Appropriators who violate operational rules are to be assessed graduated sanctions (depending on the seriousness and context of the offense) by other appropriators, by officials who are accountable to these appropriators, or by both.

(6) *Conflict-resolution mechanisms*. Appropriators and their officials have rapid access to low-cost local arenas to resolve conflicts among appropriators or between them and officials.

(7) *Recognition of rights to organize*. The rights of appropriators to devise their own institutions are not challenged by external government authorities.

(8) *Nested enterprises*. For CPRs like CAMPFIRE that are parts of larger systems, the activities of appropriation, provision, monitoring, enforcement, conflict resolution, and governance are organized in multiple layers of nested enterprises.

The minimal recognition by African governments of local communities' right to organize and define their own institutions for natural resource and wildlife management is the fundamental policy principle that inhibits co-management possibilities at present. The success or failure of common property resource management has to do with the exclusion and regulation of joint use (Berkes, 1989). The chances of success for local-level management depend critically on legitimization and support by central government. This support is lacking in sub-Saharan Africa at present. No amount of lip service to community involvement will substitute for the need to empower groups with the "right of access" to definite resources, in bounded spaces institutionally established and integrated into a regional planning framework.

Local Institutional Development

The levels of decision-making, from individual, household, village, community (local), on to district and provincial (regional) and national and international, need to be nested and united in common purpose. The benefits inherent in maintaining diversity and stability in ecosystem conservation should not be the object of conflict, particularly between higher and lower levels in the decision-making process.

Rather than a hierarchy, the decision and action process should be seen from an individual perspective of concentric circles. Each circle of participation represents an institution (household, village, community, district) that embodies some kind of collective action (Uphoff, 1986). The benefits of the institutions are "public goods," and it is suggested that the natural resource base should be perceived as the natural capital of the economic dimension of the institution.

In this conceptual framework the protected area asserts a force primarily for the local public good but also balances local interests with those of a wider public and of future generations. Only through the evolution of viable local natural-resource-management institutions will the greater public, through its agencies, be able to establish a network of co-management institutions capable of not only planning but managing a wider landscape than the park.

A way exists to maintain Africa's splendid large-mammal diversity in savanna land use by facilitating the establishment of local wildlife-management systems, linked together and with the government-protected areas. Governments should not only discuss trade-offs outside the park but realize the necessity for trade-offs inside as well. The buffer zone is not outside the park but between the perceptions of central government and local people regarding appropriate use of local resources.

132

Sustained Use

Most consumptive use of wildlife in Africa is defined by governments as illegal. While efforts to protect endangered species with force are important and heroic at times, they should not hide a profound malady of approach. While all common-pool resources need protection from illegal appropriation, the loss of Africa's elephants and rhinos in the past decades is symptomatic of a massive divide in perception of value between governments and local people.

While Western governments may believe they can protect the remnants of their wildlife diversity by the investment of enforceable regulations, it is unlikely that Africa can invest the management cost. Wildlife has to save itself, and the experience of Zimbabwe and other countries indicates that it can, provided it is used wisely and marketed effectively and the rents are appropriated to the land they came from. It is a gross tragedy that elephants and rhinos, for example, have paid so much and received so little protection in return.

Respect and care for the community of life includes improvement in the quality of human life, the conservation of the earth's vitality and diversity, and the sustained use of renewable resources (IUCN, 1991). An African conservation ethic is necessary, and it is proposed that it be based on local proprietorship and sustained use, with protected areas providing a local subsidy to ensure harmony between protected and public lands. This in turn will require governments to empower their rural people at the expense of urban people. Some communities will come off better than others. CAMPFIRE does not argue for equity but for socioeconomic justice. Those who pay the costs of having wildlife on their land must receive the economic benefit. There must be an incentive for having wildlife instead of goats and cows on the range, and it must be competitive or complementary. As McNeely (1988) states, behavior affecting the maintenance of biological diversity can best be changed by providing new approaches to conservation that alter people's perceptions of what behavior is in their self-interest.

McNeely goes on to say that unfortunately too little biodiversity will be conserved by market forces alone, and that effective government intervention is required. What "effective government intervention" is, how it will be paid for, and why it is lacking, are issues not generally stated. How are conservation costs to be met and by whom, if not by the people on the land and the countries they live in themselves?

A Caring Partnership

Maintenance of biodiversity depends on the integration of social, biotic, and economic factors. The future requires a new approach to basic needs that encompasses physical and emotional human needs as well as to maintain the ecosystems that sustains them. Governments must help rural people get back in touch with the natural resources in their areas and, on the basis of unequivocal local proprietorship, begin to reestablish a true spirit of stewardship. That spirit must translate into the process of institution-building for wildlife and natural-resource management.

The role of the state is to facilitate this process by ensuring an enabling framework and professional technical inputs. The role of science is to support the planning, training, monitoring, and evaluation phases of the policy process. The nature of the economic system for management is critical and should be determined locally, not bureaucratically, to ensure the full impact of the incentive structure. Investments must be made in developing the human institutions and understanding the ecosystem, its resources, and their use and market. Rents from the resource must be returned to the land through wise and gentle management and to the community. Managing the local environment must reward itself, and communities can determine and negotiate the rates for reinvestment (capital), sustainability (recurrent), income, community development, levies, taxes, etc.

The post-colonial synthesis proposed seeks to reunite old and new, local and central, cultural and natural diversity, in the context of modern Africa. To make co-management strategies possible, governments should be persuaded that the proposal is favorable to their own interests and does not threaten established decision-making processes. The affective economy, described by Hyden (1983), of networks of land, kinship, and support in much of rural Africa still offers a high human quality of life to many. The quality of all rural life could be lifted further by forest and wildlife departments' moving from being protectionist to becoming enablers of sustainable conservation and development.

Rural wildlife or natural-resource cooperatives could be allowed to negotiate with the national and international private sector on marketing the sustained yield from their common system. The possibility exists of regional and national associations supporting primary producers, able to capture the best possible values for their natural resource products. These resources are in some cases more valuable than others and include beautiful landscapes, lake shores, rivers, and forests as well as valuable minerals (gold, gemstones, etc.). In other areas resources are stressed by overuse. CAMPFIRE argues that you cannot generally subsidize one area from another. Spectacular resources like Victoria Falls contradict this view but reinforce the point that governments through their parks, forests, and powers can wield immense influence on local and regional land-use practices. Government need only empower people to manage their own resources and use the protected areas to supply further benefits in order to be a lead stakeholder in the policy-making for landscape planning. As it stands, the natural-resource departments in communal lands are far behind other agencies in extension services. Wildlife conservationists must participate in the development process armed with sound technical advice as to how to sustain the benefit flow.

References

Berkes, D., *et al.* 1989. "The Benefits of the Commons." *Nature*, vol. 340, 13 July. pp 91-93.

Brown, M. 1991. *Buffer Zone Management in Africa.* Paper presented to a workshop organized by the PVO/NGO/NRMS Project. (QEP, Uganda, 1990). Washington, D.C. World Wildlife Fund.

Child, B. 1991. "Wildlife Use on Zimbabwe's Rangelands." In *Developing World Agriculture, Animal Production and Health.* Hong Kong. Grosvenor Press International.

Cousins, B. 1987. *A Survey of Current Grazing Schemes in the Communal Lands of Zimbabwe.* Harare. University of Zimbabwe, Centre for Applied Social Sciences.

Cumming, D.H.M. 1990. *Wildlife Conservation in African Parks: Progress, Problems and Prescriptions.* Harare. WWF Multispecies Production Systems Project. (Project paper no. 15)

Holleman, J.F. 1969. Chief, Council and Commissioner. Royal van Gorcum. Personal communication.

Hyden, G. 1983. *No Short Cuts to Progress: African Development Management in Perspective.* Berkeley. University of California Press.

IUCN/UNEP/WWF. 1991. *Caring for the Earth: A Strategy for Sustainable Living*. Gland, Switzerland. World Conservation Union.

Martin, R.B. 1986. *CAMPFIRE: The Communal Area Management Programme for Indigenous Resources*. Harare, Zimbabwe. Ministry of Environment, Branch of Terrestrial Ecology, Department of National Parks and Wildlife Management.

McNeely, J.A. 1988. *Economics and Biological Diversity*. Gland, Switzerland. International Union for the Conservation of Nature and Natural Resources.

Murphree, M.W. 1991. *Communities as Institutions for Resource Management*. Harare. University of Zimbabwe, Centre for Applied Social Sciences.

Murphree, M.W., and D.H.M. Cumming. 1990. *Savanna Land Use: Policies and Practice in Zimbabwe*. Harare. University of Zimbabwe. (CASS/WWF Multispecies Project)

Ostrom, E. 1990. *Governing the Commons: The Evolution of Institutions for Collective Action*. New York. Cambridge University Press.

Shaffer, Mark. 1987. "Minimum Viable Populations: Coping with Uncertainty in Viable Populations for Conservation." In Michael Soulé (ed.), *Viable Populations for Conservation*. New York. Cambridge University Press. pp. 69-86.

Soulé, Michael. 1985. "What is Conservation Biology? *BioScience*, vol. 35, no. 11. pp. 727-734.

Uphoff, N., *et al.* 1986. *Local Institutional Development: An Analytical Sourcebook of Cases*. West Hartford, Ct. Kumarian Press.

Western, D., and Mary Pearl. 1989. *Conservation for the Twenty First Century*. New York. Oxford University Press.

Wilcox, Bruce A. 1980. "Insular Ecology and Conservation." In Michael E. Soulé and Bruce A. Wilcox (eds.), *Conservation Biology: An Evolutionary Ecological Perspective*. Sunderland, Mass. Sinauer Assoc. pp. 95-117.

Chapter 12

CONCLUSIONS AND RECOMMENDATIONS

Richard A. Meganck and
Richard E. Saunier

Introduction

In dealing with social concerns and biodiversity conservation in a regional context, we face the challenge of narrowing the definition of the problem, since all phases of planning involve the concerns of people. Thus, in discussions involving people from a number of disciplines the tendency is to expand the scope of the problem as linkages are noted--the result of which is a quagmire of advice which is far too broad to be effectively implemented. While the conclusions and recommendations presented here attempt to represent areas of concern routinely faced by planners they also represent concerns for biodiversity conservation.

The chapter is organized into four main sections, all relating to the value of the new regional planning as a way to address the complex issues involved in conserving biodiversity: (a) social concerns, (b) political will, (c) information, and (d) development planning. Each of these is summarized in a series of "principles" organized around a given concern of biodiversity conservation. Although they do not represent a comprehensive statement on the new regional planning, they do indicate that this methodology can contribute to the *in-situ* conservation and *ex-situ* maintenance of biodiversity. Their use will help ensure the long-term viability of these resources for all concerned parties--scientists, politicians, planners, managers, local residents, and resource users.

Social Concerns and Biodiversity Conservation

The often-repeated principle that protected areas cannot be planned in isolation from their surroundings leads to the question of what constitutes a "region." Discussions center on the impact a protected area has on its surroundings and on the impact that economic activity often has on the integrity of a protected area. Two conclusions are relevant to this question:

(1) Integrated regional development planning provides an effective framework for addressing social and economic concerns for biodiversity conservation regardless of scale or of the complexity of the region; and

(2) While the interactions between a protected area and its region are unique, the principles offered by integrated regional development planning can help to ensure that the benefits and costs of decisions concerning biodiversity conservation are fully evaluated in the planning process.

Questions are often voiced as to whether it would be preferable to establish a protected area first, and therefore influence the development process in its surrounding region, or to formulate a regional plan that included projects to establish protected areas along with other development activities. In one sense, given the concern for biodiversity, the "protected area first" choice is logical. On the other hand, since people are to be the ultimate beneficiaries of development planning they are the prime concern of the decision-making process, and therefore protected areas should not receive preferential treatment. However, the urgency in biodiversity conservation lies with those areas under pressure for unstructured development. Likewise, given the incipient state of our knowledge on biodiversity, planners may indeed have the opportunity to plan conservation areas more frequently if development planning places a priority on financing mechanisms to support basic field research as part of the planning process and if long-term public involvement in biodiversity conservation is based on an understanding of its benefits. Three principles are relevant here:

(3) Resource planners and managers should identify areas that are important to biodiversity conservation and consider the potential development activities that would affect these areas of interest.

(4) Community development activities identified in long-range plans should reflect an understanding of the direct relationship between a region's economic viability and maintenance of its biodiversity, whether included in a protected area or not.

(5) Planners and decision-makers should be aware of the issues in the region of influence of a protected area as a basis for actively engaging and involving local communities in planning and implementing biodiversity conservation measures.

The long-term viability of local economies (as opposed to project financing) can depend on the benefits and costs of having a protected area nearby. The rights of indigenous peoples, for example, often suffer because of biodiversity conservation efforts that are neither locally initiated nor accepted. Two principles can be cited here:

(6) Local resource users who live near protected areas often require support to establish effective institutions capable of influencing and participating in political, economic, and conservation decisions that affect the viability of both the protected area and the local community.

(7) Governments at all levels should consider institutional arrangements and policies to ensure information exchange, participation, and equal distribution of the economic costs and benefits to communities that depend directly on the resources available from a protected area--particularly when decisions are taken that would negatively affect a local community for the benefit of a larger population (region, nation, world). Such arrangements should include the creation of management structures having legal standing and authority that will allow full participation by populations that have historically used the protected area.

Problems for tourism and fisheries often center on the social and economic issues related to an influx of migrants to territories bordering a protected area. Sound commercial investments, though welcomed, can have direct negative impacts on the make-up of a community. Likewise, an unexpected influx of unskilled workers can affect both the local communities and the very viability of tourism based on natural amenities. A special case has to do with fishermen and the management of marine and coastal biodiversity and protected areas.

(8) When development of a protected area results in an influx of migrant workers, their social welfare should be considered. State or national government must bear the responsibility of providing basic services for these people or the future of the protected area can easily be threatened.

(9) The development of coastal and marine protected areas can affect access to established fishing areas and the use of traditional fishing methods. Compensation to local fishermen should be considered as part of the costs of implementation.

(10) Often fisheries, tourism, and conservation of marine biodiversity can not only co-exist but be mutually beneficial as well. For example, local fishermen can be valuable sources of information and loyal employees of the conservation authority. Every effort should therefore be made to involve local fishermen in planning marine and coastal reserves.

Political Will and Biodiversity Conservation

Plans are often made that, no matter how well formulated in a technical sense, are not implemented. Many reasons can be given for the archives full of unimplemented plans, including those for what have come to be referred to as "paper parks": a lack of funding, a change in development priorities, a change in political winds of a given nation or region. Sometimes, even after implementation begins, a project fails to fully produce what had been expected by the interest groups that supported it or is not fully accepted by the local community or even by the supposed beneficiaries. The reason often given for such failures is "lack of political will." Several observations, conclusions, and recommendations can be mentioned concerning this phenomenon:

(11) The desire and commitment (political will) of a decision-maker to support a proposed project is neither automatic nor predictable; it must be nurtured from the outset. Getting a decision-maker to accept a proposal is the responsibility of the planner, and therefore creating the atmosphere for its acceptance should be very high on the planning agenda.

(12) Political decisions are complex and potentially conflictive with a number of things, including the conscience and aspirations of the decision-maker, the mandates from his or her constituencies, the desires of the groups who have given financial support, the needs of the opposition, and the beliefs of his or her peers, besides the extant legislative

directives, policies, and regulations. The decision will be taken according to what the decision-maker believes to be the route of minimal conflict with the more important of these.

(13) Minimizing conflicts while meeting stated goals and objectives is a function of the new regional planning. It is done through an iterative process that is integrated across sectors, is transparent and participatory, and seeks consensus from the affected parties.

(14) Educating the decision-maker and the varying constituencies from the very outset greatly facilitates agreement on what a strategy or plan should contain. Building stakeholder pride and ownership helps to assure implementation and long-term viability.

(15) Feedback mechanisms from local communities should be developed and nurtured. These provide valuable information to both the planning team and the decision-maker. Although this type of input is unwelcome in some cultures, its acceptance is increasing and should be cultivated.

(16) There are inevitably "winners" and "losers" in any planning process. The decision-maker must be confident that the interests of all affected groups have been addressed in the strategy or plan.

(17) Building a degree of flexibility into a strategy or plan can also help to ensure the support of the decision-maker. A "perfect plan" may simply be unattainable in a political sense. Therefore, both the planning team and the decision-maker must have alternative courses of action in the event that any one issue begins to threaten the viability of the project.

Information and Biodiversity Conservation

The availability of information is fundamental to any process that would lead to effective biodiversity conservation. Without comprehensive and credible information, constituencies cannot be built or objectives attained. However, although data gathering is a task that is never completed and planning must contend with incomplete information, every effort to keep it accurate, relevant, and current must be made. Therefore,

(18) Wide-ranging consultations should be held at an early stage in the planning process to identify interested parties and obtain their views on key issues that must be addressed by the planning team.

(19) All involved and affected parties, including governments and corporations, have a responsibility to make relevant information available to the planning team as a means of ensuring the broadest possible debate on the decision as to how a given site should be managed.

(20) All information collected by the planning team must be accessible to any group with legitimate interests in the outcome of the planning effort.

(21) The information collected should be widely inclusive: technical, scientific, local, and traditional.

(22) Information used by the planning team should include the historical, natural, and cultural aspects to learn from past experience in planning and managing for the future.

Development Planning and Biodiversity Conservation

Protected areas interact with their surrounding region in two ways: (a) they play an essential part in its economic development, and (b) the protection of their resources depends on their proper management in the widest possible regional context. Once a decision is made to establish a protected area, concern for its long-term health is fundamental to any community that hopes to realize long-term benefits from the arrangement. A number of conclusions and recommendations treat this subject.

(23) Clear definition of the specific role that a protected area should play in a region or national development policy is of vital importance to ensure that it provides the wished-for range of goods and services over the long term.

(24) Realizing the full potential of a protected area, regardless of its stated goals, requires the development of linkages with other sectors of society. Protected areas cannot exist without people.

(25) Interactions between a protected area and other ongoing or proposed development activities, such as mining, forestry, agriculture, fisheries, and urban development, need to be clearly identified.

(26) Effective systems for gathering, storing, and communicating information bring together the various partners and constituents of a planning exercise. They are essential for providing maximum benefits to the community.

Contributors

Juan José Castro-Chamberlain. Since 1978 Juan José Castro has worked with the Organization of American States, for which he is currently international co-director of technical cooperation on the La Amistad Biosphere Reserve projects in Costa Rica and Panama. He holds a B.S. degree in agricultural economics and international agricultural development from Cornell University (1965) and an M.S. degree in natural-resources development from the Centro Americano de Tecnología, Investigación y Educación (CATIE) in Turrialba, Costa Rica. Previously, he was with the U.S. Agency for International Development mission to Costa Rica and served as an associate director and program training officer for the U.S. Peace Corps program in Costa Rica. He has had private-sector experience as manager of Xerox and Copicentro and with Orlich Coffee production enterprises in Costa Rica. From 1970 until 1978 he was an associate professor in the School of Agricultural Economics of the University of Costa Rica.

Nina Chambers. Nina Chambers received an M.S. in wildland management from the University of Idaho. Her experience includes the design and implementation of conservation and community development projects associated with protected areas throughout Central America and in Jamaica. The main emphasis of her work has been in buffer-zone design and management, which emphasized the participation of rural villagers. Currently, she lives in northern New Mexico and is continuing conservation work for wild places and rural communities under the auspices of Round River Conservation Studies.

Joshua C. Dickinson III. Dr. Dickinson is executive vice president of Tropical Research and Development, an environmental management and land-use consultant firm operating world-wide. He is also founder and executive director of The Tropical Forest Management Trust Inc., a non-governmental organization dedicated to fostering sound management of tropical forests. Dr. Dickinson holds a B.S. degree in engineering from the United States Naval Academy and M.A. and doctoral degrees in geography from the University of Florida in Gainesville. He did postdoctoral work at the Institute of Ecology at the University of Georgia and with the Organization for Tropical Studies. From 1967 to 1972 he was assistant director of the Center for Tropical Agriculture and assistant professor of geography at the University of Florida. He has lived in Brazil, Venezuela, Peru, and Honduras and has traveled to many countries of the world over the past 25 years of professional work in environmental management.

Dennis Glick. Dennis Glick is an associate program director with the Greater Yellowstone Coalition, Bozeman, Montana, where he has been responsible for planning and directing the Greater Yellowstone Tomorrow project, which included the development of a Blueprint for sustaining the Greater Yellowstone Ecosystem. Previously he served as the co-director of the Wildlands and Human Needs Program of the World Wildlife Fund and as WWF's Central American program officer. He has worked throughout Central America on wildlands and wildlife-related issues at CATIE and as a park planner for the Government of Honduras. He has consulted on numerous occasions on these issues in North, Central, and South America and is the author of numerous popular articles, journal publications, and planning documents. Mr. Glick holds a B.S. from the School of Forestry of Oregon State University and an M.S. from the School of Natural Resources of the University of Michigan.

Sam H. Ham. Dr. Sam Ham is professor of environmental communication and international conservation at the University of Idaho, where he teaches wildland interpretation, environmental education, international nature conservation, and ecotourism management. He has conducted training workshops in twenty countries throughout North, Central, and South America and is the author of more than eighty publications, including two widely acclaimed books on interpretative methods. He has served as senior editor of the *Journal of Interpretation*, and as National Research Chair for the National Association for Interpretation (NAI). He has received the University of Idaho's Outstanding Teacher Award, its Alumni Award for Faculty Excellence, and its Award for Teaching Excellence. In 1990 he was made an NAI Fellow and in 1992 was appointed to the IUCN Commission on Education and Communication.

Edwin E. Krumpe. Dr. Krumpe is professor of resource recreation and tourism at the University of Idaho and principal scientist of wilderness management and director of the University's Wilderness Research Center. He has over fifteen years of teaching and research experience in

146

recreation and tourism management, wilderness and wild and scenic river planning, and public involvement and conflict management. During this period he has studied the preferences of park visitors, river floaters, and powerboaters for river-management strategies and the perceptions of conflict among the different types of users. He has recently specialized in designing public meetings where people can freely express their ideas based upon informed opinions in a non-threatening atmosphere. Dr. Krumpe is the author of numerous publications dealing with the management of parks and protected areas and other wildland preserves.

Lynn McCoy. Ms. McCoy is co-founder of Sustainable Decisions, Inc., a natural-resource planning firm based in Moscow, Idaho, which specializes in bringing together resource managers and members of the community to collaborate on park management direction. She has broad experience in public involvement as applied to natural resource management and has worked with diverse groups and agencies to help them solve conflicts and reach agreement on a variety of wilderness, wild and scenic river, and park plans. Ms. McCoy specializes in the application of the Limits of Acceptable Change (LAC) planning system, a framework for establishing acceptable and appropriate ecological, social, and administrative conditions. Her research findings and conflict-resolving techniques have been presented at national and international conferences including the Vth World Wilderness Congress, in Norway, and the IVth World Congress on National Parks and Protected Areas, in Venezuela.

Jeffrey A. McNeely. Mr. McNeely is the director of the Biodiversity Programme of the World Conservation Union (IUCN) in Switzerland, where he has worked for twelve years. Previously he had worked in Southeast Asia for twelve years, contributing to a wide range of conservation activities for governments, United Nations agencies, and private conservation organizations in Thailand, Indonesia, and Nepal. He is the author or editor of nearly twenty books, including *Conserving the World's Biological Diversity; Parks for Life; Mammals of Thailand; Culture and Conservation; National Parks, Conservation, and Development; Economics and Biological Diversity; People and Protected Areas in the Hindu-Kush Himalaya; Mammals of the Palaearctic Deserts;* and *Soul of the Tiger.* More than 100 of his technical articles and 150 of his popular articles have been published. He serves on the editorial advisory committee of several journals, including *Environmental Conservation, Parks, Oryx, Biodiversity and Conservation, Tomorrow,* and *Sustainable Development.*

Arturo Martínez. Dr. Martínez is the senior programme officer in the Secretariat of the Convention on Biological Diversity. Before coming to that position in 1993, he was the expert member in the Argentine delegation during the negotiation of the Convention and a member of the panel of experts established by the United Nations Environmental Programme (UNEP) to follow up on it. From 1990 to 1993 he was Director of the Biological Resources Institute (INTA) in Argentina, which is the responsible for the management of *ex-situ* collections of genetic resources for food and agriculture. During that time he was also the Coordinator of the Southern Cone Regional Program (Argentina, Bolivia, Brazil, Paraguay, and Uruguay) of the Inter-American Center for Cooperation on Agriculture (IICA) for the collection, evaluation, and conservation of genetic resources for food and agriculture. His doctoral degree is from the University of Reading and the Royal Botanical Gardens at Kew in the field of plant biosystematics.

Richard A. Meganck. Richard Meganck is director of the International Environmental Technology Center of UNEP. Previously he served as the director of the UNEP Regional Seas Programme in the Wider Caribbean and as director and regional UNEP representative for Asia and the Pacific. Dr. Meganck began his career in the mid-1970s as a faculty member in the College of Forestry at Oregon State University and currently holds courtesy professorships at several universities. Before joining UNEP he worked for thirteen years in the inter-American system at the Organization of American States and the Inter-American Development Bank. He has published widely on a number of subjects, including protected-area planning and management, climate change, and environmental education. He holds a B.Sc. and M.Sc. in watershed management and resource development and policy from Michigan State University and a Ph.D. in natural-resource management from Oregon State University.

Simon Metcalfe. Simon Metcalfe is research associate at the Centre for Applied Social Science in the Natural Resource Management Programme at the University of Zimbabwe and adviser to the Zimbabwe Trust's program supporting CAMPFIRE. He holds a degree in political science with special reference to Africa from the University of Zimbabwe and was a Hubert Humphrey Fellow at Cornell University in 1991 and 1992. He was an urban social and community worker in Britain and has worked in community development and primary health care in rural Zimbabwe, where he was field director of the Save the Children Fund (UK). Since 1988 he has been involved in community-based wildlife management and was the inaugural manager of the Nyaminyami Wildlife Management Trust and of the National Campfire Association of Wildlife Producing Communities. He is currently analyzing linkages between CAMPFIRE's emphasis on wildlife and other natural resources, with special emphasis on land tenure, and advising on enhanced resource-management training for community-based institutions.

William J. Possiel. William Possiel is vice president and director of the Brazil Regional Program of The Nature Conservancy (TNC). He has sixteen years of domestic and international experience in forestry, environmental education, and natural-resource management and currently administers four landscape-scale conservation initiatives in Brazil. He provides direction for the Conservancy's national and international efforts through participation on the TNC Conservation Committee. He lived in Brazil for two years working on the development of the Atlantic Forest Bioreserve and advising TNC on the development of the Brazil Program. Prior to this, he was Ohio state director for TNC where he completed a $11.5 million campaign to protect critical natural areas in Ohio and Latin America. He holds a B.S. in management science from Kean College, New Jersey, and a B.S. in forestry and an M.A. in anthropology from Oregon State University.

Manuel Ramírez. Manuel Ramírez is the country program director for Conservation International in Costa Rica and Panama, where he is in charge of its program of technical cooperation in the La Amistad Biosphere Reserve in both countries. He has ten years of experience working with the Tropical Science Center in natural-resource management projects throughout Latin America and has participated in technical assistance projects as a consultant in natural-resource management for the World Bank, UNDP, the Swedish International Development Agency, the Canadian International Development Agency, and the Andean Development Corporation, among others. In 1982 he received a degree in forestry engineering from the Instituto Tecnológico de Costa Rica and in 1988 an M.F. from Yale University.

Richard E. Saunier. Richard E. Saunier is the senior environmental management adviser in the Department of Regional Development and Environment of the Organization of American States, where he has worked since 1975. Previously, 1970-1975, he held staff positions with the U.S. Peace Corps in Paraguay, Peru, and Washington, D.C., and during 1967-1969 he was visiting professor of forestry at the Universidad Austral de Chile in Valdivia, Chile. He holds a B.S. degree from Colorado State University in forestry and range management and M.S. and Ph.D. degrees in range ecology and watershed management from the University of Arizona. Dr. Saunier is a member of the IUCN Commission on Environmental Strategy and Planning and of the Board of Directors of Planning Assistance, a non-profit group that gives management assistance to private voluntary organizations working in family planning and food production.

D. Scott Slocombe. Dr. Slocombe is an associate professor in the Department of Geography of Wilfrid Laurier University, Waterloo, Canada, and past director of the WLU Cold Regions Research Centre. His research interests are in ecosystem-based planning and management, ecosystem and landscape modeling, nonequilibrium systems theories, sustainability, and environmental reporting and information systems. He received a B.I.S. in ecology and environmental studies from the University of Waterloo, an M.Sc. in regional and resources planning from the University of British Columbia, and a Ph.D. in regional and environmental planning from the University of Waterloo. He is actively involved with several NGOs: as a member of the IUCN Commission on Environmental Strategy and Planning, as Vice-Chair of the new Canadian Network for Environmental Education and Communication, and as a member of the board of the North American Association for Environmental Education.